The Male Ordeal

The Male Ordeal

Role Crisis in a Changing World

Eric Skjei, Ph.D.
and
Richard Rabkin, M.D.

G. P. Putnam's Sons
New York

Copyright © 1981 by Eric Skjei and Richard Rabkin
All rights reserved. This book, or parts thereof, may not be reproduced in any form without permission in writing from the publisher.
Published simultaneously in Canada by Academic Press Canada, Limited, Toronto.

The authors gratefully acknowledge permission from the following sources to reprint material in this book:

Beacon Press for material from *One-Dimensional Man* by Herbert Marcuse, copyright © 1964 by Herbert Marcuse.

Doubleday & Co., Inc., for material from *Women and Madness* by Phyllis Chesler, copyright © 1972 by Phyllis Chesler; from *Sexual Politics* by Kate Millett, copyright © 1969, 1970 by Kate Millett; and from *The Brain: The Last Frontier* by Richard M. Restak, M.D., copyright © 1979 by Richard M. Restak.

Lindsy Van Gelder for material from "An Unmarried Man," *Ms.*, November 1979.

Herb Goldberg for material from *The Hazards of Being Male*, Signet 1977.

Grove Press, Inc., for material from *The Wretched of the Earth* by Frantz Fanon, copyright © 1968 by Frantz Fanon.

Harcourt Brace Jovanovich, Inc., for material from *Totalitarianism* by Hannah Arendt, copyright © 1968 by Hannah Arendt.

Harper & Row, Publishers, Inc., for material from *The Future of Marriage* by Jessie Bernard (The World Publishing Company), copyright © 1972 by Jessie Bernard; from *The Mermaid and the Minotaur* by Dorothy Dinnerstein, copyright © 1976 by Dorothy Dinnerstein; and from *The True Believer* by Eric Hoffer, copyright © 1951 by Eric Hoffer.

Alfred A. Knopf, Inc., for material from *Crazy Salad: Some Things About Women* by Nora Ephron, copyright © 1975 by Nora Ephron; from *Type A Behavior and Your Heart* by Meyer Friedman and Ray H. Rosenman, copyright © 1974 by Meyer Friedman and Ray H. Rosenman; and from *The Feminized Male: Classrooms, White Collars, and the Decline of Manliness* by Patricia Cayo Sexton, copyright © 1969 by Patricia Cayo Sexton.

McGraw-Hill Book Co. for material from *The Male Machine* by Marc Feigen Fasteau, copyright © 1974 by Marc F. Fasteau.

Dr. John Money and California Institute of Technology for material from "Matched Pairs of Hermaphrodites: Behavioral Biology of Sexual Differentiation from Chromosomes to Gender Identity," by John Money, reprinted from *Engineering and Science*, April 1970. Published at The California Institute of Technology.

William Morrow & Co., Inc., for material from *The Dialectic of Sex* by Shulamith Firestone, copyright © 1970 by Shulamith Firestone; from *The*

New Male by Herb Goldberg, copyright © 1979 by Herb Goldberg; from *Coming of Age in Samoa* by Margaret Mead, copyright © 1928, 1955 by Margaret Mead; and from *Male and Female* by Margaret Mead, copyright © 1949 by the author.

Newsweek for material from "How Men are Changing," January 16, 1978.

W. W. Norton & Co., Inc., and Virago Publishing, Ltd., for material from *Of Woman Born* by Adrienne Rich, copyright © 1976 by Adrienne Rich.

Opinion Publications, Inc., and the authors for material from "The Abandoned Husband: When Wives Leave" by Ellen Halle; for "The Decline of Manhood: Adaptive Trend or Temporary Confusion?" by Wolfgang Lederer, M.D.; and for "Women in the Labor Force: Some Mental Health Implications" by Doreen E. Schecter, M.D. All three articles appeared in *Psychiatric Opinion*.

The Seabury Press, Inc., for material from *Pedagogy of the Oppressed* by Paulo Friere, copyright © 1970 by the author.

Graham B. Spanier and Randie Margolis for material from "Marital Quality, Marital Stability, and Extramarital Sexual Behavior," paper presented at the annual meeting of the International Academy of Sex Research, August 21, 1979, Prague, Czechoslovakia.

Terry S. Stein, M.D., for material from "The Effects of the Women's Movement on Men: A Therapist's View" by Terry S. Stein, an address delivered to the 1979 annual meeting of the American Psychiatric Association.

United Press International for material from "Stress Can Cause a Loss of Interest in Sex Appetite," by Patricia McCormack, in the *Oakland Tribune*, November 12, 1979.

Universal Press Syndicate for excerpts from Richard Reeves's interview with Betty Friedan, copyright © 1979 by Universal Press Syndicate.

Library of Congress Cataloging in Publication Data

Skjei, Eric W.
    The male ordeal.

    Bibliography: p.
    Includes index.
    1. Men—United States. 2. Men—United States—Psychology.
3. Feminism—United States. I. Rabkin, Richard, 1932–   . II. Title.
HQ1090.3.S54   1981   305.3   81-5175
ISBN 0-399-12575-2   AACR2

PRINTED IN THE UNITED STATES OF AMERICA

To
All those men and women who responded to our questions with such warm and generous candor

For
Roger, Ann, Karen, Susan, and, no doubt, Henry.
—E.S.

Contents

	Preface	11
I	The Male Dilemma	21
II	Studying and Portraying Men's Reactions to the Women's Movement	40
III	Men Respond: The Interviews	62
IV	Ordeal or Challenge?	221
	Notes	242
	A Reading List for Men	246

Preface

THIS BOOK is about men. It is about the curious blend in the male psyche of confident self-assurance and profound emotional hunger. It is about the power of the masculine drive to build stable, harmonious relationships with others, checked by an equally powerful fear of rejection. It is about the value of masculinity, and our need to restore our common appreciation of it.

Because this is a book about men, it is also inevitably a book about women, and about the nature of the alliances and conflicts between them. Above all, it is about the strong but generally unanalyzed impact that the last two decades of resurgent American feminism has had on men.

Our thesis in *The Male Ordeal* is that the women's movement has altered and will continue to substantially alter men's roles as well as those of women, a fact that in the fifteen years or so of feminist reforms has never been fully acknowledged. We wish we could say that it has been both a women's and a men's movement, one in which both sexes have worked together to change the way in which they interact with each other. However, while women have acted and created an essentially powerful and progressive cultural force, men have too often just reacted, mostly in silent crisis or, as the title suggests, as if they were enduring an ordeal.

As men begin belatedly to try to make sense of the changes in women, as they begin to try to adjust to the effect of these changes on their own roles and self-images, many experience significant psychological stress. The men we have interviewed describe feelings of frustration and bewilderment, pain and anger. The emergence of feminine autonomy holds unpredictable, threatening overtones for many of them. The lives of some have suffered irrevocable, catastrophic disruptions. However, those who have successfully adapted to major shifts in their role describe the process as an invaluable one, one that they are stronger for having endured.

The trauma that role reversal imposes on men is not always justified. At times, the feminist response to the male dominance of our culture becomes impatient, self-indulgent, and vindictive. A paradoxical type of gender bigotry, one that we have labeled *the new misandry* has emerged. New misandry mirrors its masculine precedents in a particularly ugly way. We discuss the phenomenon in some detail in Chapter III. More than one woman casually observed to us in the course of our interviews that she had long ago relinquished any hope of ever achieving any sort of credible psychological rapport with a man. "For support, it's women," Germaine Greer is quoted as saying. "I sleep with men. I don't expect anything else from them."[1]

Not only is this misandric attitude emerging in the relatively rarefied atmosphere of pronouncements by feminist writers, it is also subtly shaping the tools used by electronic media to fuel the machinery of mass-market enterprise:

> One ad that appeared regularly in the winter of 1979–80 on prime time network television opened with a shot of a man and woman in bed. The woman appears to be sound asleep, the man is awake. He looks miserable. He coughs, sits up, leans over, and in a plaintive voice says, "Barbara, you up? Barbara, you up?" Wearily she replies, "I

am now." Plaintively, he whines, "I don't think I can sleep with this cold. Throat's all sore." "Alright," she responds, "I'll get the aspirin and (brand name of throat lozenges)." In the next shot, she is handing him the medication. He looks like a petulant, overgrown child. In the closing shot, he's now sound asleep and she's wide awake, sitting up in bed playing solitaire. "Well," she murmurs in a tone of exasperated resignation, "I'm glad one of us can sleep."

The message here seems clear. Men are big, helpless babies that women have to make sacrifices for and take care of. They make unreasonable demands. (Why did he have to wake her up? Why couldn't he have gotten up and found the cold medicine himself?) Presumably, women watching the ad are supposed to identify with the martyred woman it portrays and go out and buy the product.

Thus men find themselves in a very strange bind. Those few who do make an active effort to understand the women's movement all too often find themselves not only rebuffed, but subtly forced to play the very role that women scorn them for: bullies, babies, compulsive achievers, sexual imperialists. Naturally, the more thoughtful among them respond by becoming more and more indifferent to feminist issues, more and more estranged, less and less prepared to respond effectively when those issues strike close to home and suddenly transform a wife or a colleague from a dependable partner into a stranger, an individual whose struggles for greater autonomy necessarily look like rejection.

If there is one word that epitomizes the common male response to issues raised in the last decade by the women's movement, issues of obvious consequence for both men and women, it is *reticence*.

The old heterosexual arrangement has become in an intimate way—a way that has to do with a person's sense of history but that throws the person privately off balance too, a way that hurts the felt inner core of individual vitality—unworkable.

Not only is this intimate hurt felt more keenly by women than it seems (at least on the surface) to be felt by men.* [Footnote: . . . I cannot judge how the men whom the breakdown affects really feel about it: women's reactions to it have been more articulate.]²

—Dorothy Dinnerstein

The women we spoke to made it clear that they consider male silence on the gender issue to be more than just noncommittal detachment. In their eyes it is just one more example of *de facto* chauvinism, a kind of discrimination by omission. They also make it clear that if it continues, men run the risk of not only being judged passively obstructive, but also of forfeiting their right to determine the way in which their own roles evolve.

We think this male silence is deceptive. Men do, as the interview extracts in this book vividly demonstrate, feel passionately involved in the issues raised by the women's movement. They have very strong feelings and opinions about what the movement represents to them, but they also recognize that these issues, precisely because they are so fundamental, are not simple and will not be instantly resolved. Furthermore, the men we spoke to were well aware of their own internal conflicts over many of these issues. They expressed an understandable desire to surmount some of this personal ambivalence before taking more public stands about these matters.

The Male Ordeal is an attempt to help explore this masculine hesitation, one that poses the danger of amplifying rather than dampening gender dissonance. Male skepticism about the significance and stamina of the women's movement may have been initially justified, but it is now time for men to accept the fact—if only because such demographic realities as the participation of well over half of all adult American women in the labor force argue it irrefutably—that the women's movement is not just another hysterical fad. Feminism may evolve, may even become relatively invisible as other events preoccupy the media and our masss consciousness, but its impact will be felt for years to come. The new orientation that women have toward their identities as women and their dignity as human beings is an implacable one. It is now up to men to make it clear that the historical drive to expand the conditions of human emancipation is not one that can in any way progress without the full involvement of both sexes.

The topic of the relationship between men and women is so vast, so intricate, so nebulous that it seems at times to defy reasonable discussion. Our remarks here are in no way intended as definitive. They are best construed as one among many contributions to a debate that, conducted in one form or another, will presumably continue unabated for some time to come. The value of the present debate, it seems, is not so much resolution as moderation and restraint. Most of the voices raised recently on gender concerns have been those of women. Now that those voices have in a sense liberated us all from our preconceptions about the natural importance of men in this culture, now that men have the unprecedented opportunity to identify with any cultural position and perspective they wish, it is time for them to be heard from again.

If any society—large or small, simple or complex, based on the most rudimentary hunting and fishing or on the whole intricate interchange of manufactured products—is to survive, it must have a pattern of social life that comes to terms with the differences between the sexes.

—Margaret Mead
Male and Female

The Male Ordeal

I

The Male Dilemma

JACK TRANER is a forty-eight-year-old lawyer who shares a thriving practice in Santa Barbara, California, with three other attorneys. A distinguished member of his profession, Traner is a senior partner in his firm, past vice-president of the California State Bar, and a prominent Democratic Party fundraiser. Liked and admired by those who know him, Traner is rumored to be in line for appointment to a judge's seat in the near future. He is also the father of two bright, ambitious daughters, aged sixteen and seventeen, both of whom are now attending the same private school in Pennsylvania.

Not long before our conversation with him, Jack had what he considered to be the perfect life: a challenging, rewarding career, the esteem of his peers, a beautiful family, and the love and affection of a warm and attractive woman, his wife Helen, to whom he was completely devoted. Without having to give it a second thought, Jack Traner sensed that he was that rare individual, an entirely happy man.

Then one day about two years ago, he came home from work to learn that Helen was leaving him. She explained that she loved him and was sorry to hurt him, but now that their children were almost grown and were leaving for school, she wanted something she had never had before in her life and knew that she needed: to be on her own, without any kind of involvement with or commitment to a man. The next day she packed her clothes and drove away. Since then Jack has seen her only three times, very briefly. They were divorced nine months after she departed.

Though Jack was deeply shocked when Helen left him, at first he was able to hold himself together, convinced that she would change her mind, would realize she didn't want to live without him, would miss him too much, and would return. When he finally forced himself to accept the fact that she was serious, that she would not be coming back to him, and that his life had been radically and permanently altered without his consent, Jack had a nervous breakdown.

> I'd wake up in the middle of the night in a cold sweat, completely drenched, shaking all over, just as though I had a severe fever. Sometimes I could remember having had a nightmare, usually one in which Helen was being murdered in one gruesome way or another, but as often as not my mind was a total blank. I didn't know where I was, who I was, anything. Definitely the worst period, psychologically, of my entire life. Without question.
>
> Then I usually couldn't get back to sleep. So after tossing and turning for what always seemed like hours, I'd finally give up and get out of bed and go out into the kitchen and make myself a stiff drink . . .
>
> That's another thing, the drinking. I was drinking a lot in those days, without even really knowing

just how much I was putting away. Every once in a while I'd notice that, you know, the scotch bottle was almost empty again, and then I'd think back and realize that I'd only bought it the morning of the day before and I'd be completely stunned to find that it had gone so fast. Honest to God, I'd try to remember if I'd had company or something, because I just couldn't believe I was putting it away so fast. But it was invariably me. I was the only one in the house, I knew that for sure, and I wasn't exactly a social lion those days, so it was me. But then I'd forget all about it and just go right on knocking 'em back.

But you can see how much of a daze I was in all that time.

Another thing, it got to the point where it was virtually impossible for me to make decisions anymore, even the most ordinary, routine ones, the ones that most people make thousands of times a day without even thinking about them. For example, I'd lie in bed for hours in the mornings, totally paralyzed, unable to make up my mind between getting up and going to the office or just saying fuck it and having my secretary cancel all my appointments again for that day.

As it was, if I did get into the office, I still couldn't really function. Other people in the office told me later that I was really out of it. They'd try to talk to me and I wouldn't respond. I'd just look right through them like they weren't there. Sometimes, at the beginning, before they started to wise up and keep me on ice, I'd go to meetings with clients, and then in the middle of the meeting, in the middle of someone's *sentence*, I'd just stand up and walk out, not saying a word to anyone.

They were absolutely flabbergasted, especially since I'd always been the crisp, businesslike, no-

nonsense type. Now I'd wind up just sitting in my office all day, staring at a draft or a memo, not really seeing it, not moving, not even really completely aware of where I was. Half the time I think I must have been crying, but I tend to block some of it out now.

Word got around the office pretty quick, and co-workers, even secretaries were coming in and asking me if I was O.K. and could they do anything for me. Then I'd shake myself out of it for a couple of hours and start on a case, get into the middle of it and then totally forget what I was doing. *I wasn't even in touch with reality enough to be scared by what was happening to me.* I was in a dreamworld, but it was a nightmare, a special kind of hell, not a dream.

Finally my boss, a shrewd old buzzard, took me aside and told me to take a vacation and straighten myself out. I had to ask him what he meant. He said, "See a shrink, dammit. You need help." He really laid it on the line.

So I got into therapy and although it started out kind of slow, it eventually did me a lot of good. The guy put me on Sinequan right away, it's an antidepressant, you take it at night and you get really sleepy. Plus you can't drink too much, which is good, or it was for me at the time. And I got into my dreams and fantasies a lot more than I ever had before. You know, all this intense emotional stuff only came out when I finally realized that Helen really meant it, that she wasn't kidding around, that she was gone for good. That was some three months or so after she first dropped the bombshell on me. Later I saw her, two or three times, for about fifteen minutes each time, and it was really too painful for me.

I couldn't believe it when she first told me. I

couldn't believe it, that I could have been so out of touch with her. All I could think for that first three months was that she'd flipped out. I kept thinking she needed to get into therapy, that she was unstable or something. I honestly believed she was nuts . . .

Well, like I say, it took being in therapy to get me to the point where I could really begin to accept it as a fact, as reality, permanent reality, that she was gone for good, that she wasn't going to be coming back, and that there wasn't a damn thing I could do about it. And once I understood that, then I had to start pulling myself together, because I sure as shit knew no one else was going to do it for me. *Then* I began to understand how completely furious I was about the whole situation. Outraged. Murderous. My fantasies were all intensely violent, full of hate and revenge. I wanted to hurt her. Scenes of her dying in a fire, or a car accident. In a way, kind of interesting, because they were the same type of fantasy scenes I'd been having earlier about myself, about suicide. Running my car into a freeway abutment, that kind of thing. A pretty obvious kind of shift when you think about it—I'd refocused my anger away from myself and on to her.

Anyway, therapy helped a lot. I was able to function again. I quit losing weight, quit crying all the time for no reason. That pain in the chest, the one I thought was some kind of coronary, disappeared—just an anxiety symptom, according to the psychiatrist. When he put me on Sinequan, it went away.

I pulled myself together, got back into my usual routines, began to feel halfway normal again. The really rough part lasted for a total of about three weeks. But it's been, let's see, two years now, and

> I still don't feel I'm completely through with it. I haven't been able to really settle into a good relationship with a woman since then, and I still feel very hesitant about getting that committed to someone again. Burned, I guess you'd call it, I feel burned.

Jack is not alone. There are many other men like him in this country, men of all ages and from all classes, men of widely different kinds of social, occupational, and educational backgrounds, men that we've had the opportunity to talk to and, in many cases, extensively interview in recent months. All of them are men who have been surprised recently by sudden, unsettling shifts in their relationships with and attitudes about women, shifts usually precipitated by women. Few of these men have suffered ruptures in their lives as abrupt or as dramatic as Jack's. The emotional upheavals that most of them encountered were not as severe as his, but their stories are all very similar. In our view, all of them are experiencing some degree of sex-role transition stress.

> In the long run, the social structure itself may be transformed by the evolving roles. Already there are fundamental changes in the relationships of men and women at work and at home. But in the process, the shift is creating some turmoil, especially among men who came of age with traditional assumptions of male primacy. Many of them are now confused to the point of anguish about what their roles should be.[1]

Many of the events that trigger sex-role transition stress in men arise from assertive, liberated women's rejection of repressive expectations or habits. For example, such a woman may refuse to make coffee for her boss, or deliberately forestall a man's attempt to interrupt her conversation, or insist on paying for her own meal in a restaurant. She may ask her husband to fix dinner on Thursday nights since she's decided to go back to school. She may decide to take a vacation by herself, or to accept a job offer in a different city.

Other forms of assertion are not so constructive. One of the women we interviewed made it a policy never to read anything that wasn't written by a woman. She was surprised by the male response to her choice. A man we spoke to described having the night before held the door open as he entered a local nightclub for whoever might be coming in behind him, only to find it was a woman who proceeded to chastise him for his sexist chivalry.

Few of the men we talked to, even those for whom sex-role transition had been particularly painful, automatically defined it as an entirely negative experience. Most conceded that some degree of male tension over a changing role is probably inevitable, particularly in a society that has been male centered for so long. Small amounts of male sex-role transition stress may even, most of these men agreed, constitute a useful learning experience.

What men *do* object to is that changes in their role are often imposed on them mistrustfully and contentiously, as if they were opponents to be bested rather than allies to be enlisted. They object to the tacit abandonment of a sense of gender partnership, one that most of them subscribe to passionately and have tried to instill into their own relationships.

As a result of this misandric bias, many men feel unfairly excluded from what they have come to believe is an important struggle for *human* rights, one in which they feel they have an equal stake with women. Whether they are literally being deserted by their wives, challenged by female co-workers, or simply confused by the many new attitudes that come across the pages of newspapers, magazines, and books, or are portrayed on tv and in films, even the most liberal, tolerant, and generous men are often left feeling unprepared to respond to the entire issue of changing sex roles with anything more positive than perplexity, silence, and ultimately, estrangement. It is an estrangement that is often disguised but never truly dispelled by noncommittal male endorsements of the broad goals of equality and liberation.

The women's movement has of course for some years now been the most visible and vocal expression of a powerful appetite for change on the part of women in general. At the threshold of the 1980's, the women's movement appears to be entering a second phase, one in which it means to make even more concrete advances in the legal, political, and economic status of women. In consolidating its past gains, the movement has managed through adroit captivation of the media to broaden its psychological base of support to the point where it can now be said to exert a significant influence on the *majority* of women in this country, even in their most personal interactions with men.

However, the movement has carried with it a tacit sense of gender separatism, one that may have been appropriate at an earlier stage, but which now poses only a potential for further aggravation of a sense of polarization and antagonism between the sexes. Both the men and the women to whom we spoke were highly sensitive to this gender schism. As we explain in more detail in Chapter III, we believe this tendency now risks becoming counterproductive. And as we explain further in Chapter III, men impress us as being interested in their own way in some kind of re-alignment of sex roles, one that will ideally allow for more genuine equality for both sexes. But they will not collaborate wholeheartedly with such a project if it is predicated on gender secessionism or on repressively polemical attitudes. Nor, we suspect, will most women.

Harold Varrick, 43, the assistant superintendent of a large unified school district in an ethnically mixed urban area in Massachusetts, is, like Jack Traner, a man who has recently had to cope with profound changes in his role, caused by his wife Lois' decision to leave him after 14 years of marriage. A large, softspoken man, Varrick has two children, Timothy, 11, and Julie, three years younger.

    I don't think women realize the power they have to make men unhappy, to victimize men, not only psychologically, but legally, economically. They have the legal clout now. They have power through discrimination cases, as well as in the divorce situation, because of the courts. I don't know how that happened, but the prejudice of the legal system is clearly on the side of the woman, as far as I can tell. Maybe it's just this country's intrinsic sense of fairness. At least on an intellectual level, we all say that's true, women have been discriminated against, but no one understands the social consequences of the implementation of certain kinds of "equality," especially in intimate personal situations. It can tear them apart.
    But it was men who passed those laws. The changes of law in the last few decades to favor women have all come from male legislators, which is something feminists tend to forget. There are still very few women in any legislature. That's wrong, and it should change, but the fact is, it was men who passed the laws that are giving women *preferential* treatment in some of these situations. Also, there is a long tradition of civil rights, of high regard for human rights in this country, and that plays a part. The country's built on the whole ideal of advancement of human rights, on a struggle for greater human freedom and "equality," which is a damned hard term to define. We've had the black struggle for equality, the struggle for unionization before that, now the women's movement is like the most recent manifestation of a long tradition of human rights struggles. As a country we just seem

to take very seriously the whole idea of personal freedom and equality. There is some kind of fundamental principle of emancipation built into the social and political fabric of this country. That's a very good thing, but in intense personal situations, like marriage, when you introduce those political perspectives, you have to do so gently, or you do a great deal of damage. Some women don't realize that. They think they have to break away. They start to see all men as The Oppressor, they dehumanize men, and pretty soon men are having to bear the brunt of their revolution. I feel a little sad, I feel puzzled by that whole thing. How did we wind up being the kind of scapegoats for all the things that women are objecting to in their lives?

Furthermore, it seems to me that it's men in the middle class that really get it in the neck. It's those of us who are *not* at the extremes of power, wealth, and class that get it. The extremes are not so affected by the women's movement, or not in the same way. Anything in the middle is vulnerable. The poor can't deal with it because they're trying to eat and put a roof over their heads, and raise their kids. And the rich own too much of the system for a woman to walk away from it. They work it out other ways: property settlements, or they say, "Oh well it doesn't matter because I take a vacation for half the year anyway and we're apart so what the hell do I have to escape from?"

In my own personal case, I think the thing that makes me angriest is that I had no choice. There was no attempt to work it out, to work it through. It was all handed to me in an ultimatum, unilaterally. My wife and I had a good relationship, we were able to talk about things, to share our feelings, but when it came to this issue, she just made up her mind in a vacuum and then dropped the whole ball of wax in my lap. That I really resent. It's damned insensitive, and it turned us into adversaries in a way we never really were before. Now all it's left me with is the determination to never let myself be used that way by anyone again. It's a partnership all the way down the line or it's nothing, and I know other men who feel the same way.

For days after she told me she wanted a divorce, I kept saying, "Look, let's explore this together, let's talk it over, let's get counseling." Her answer always was, "No, I don't want to learn how to live better with you. I don't want to save the marriage. I want to be on my own. There really isn't anything to talk about." But, damn it, there was: my feelings about it, if nothing else.

So anything that she thought would be an obstacle to her being on her own, counseling, working out problems, all that, she wasn't having any of it. She killed something that we both held in common, and now I'm paying for it. That's made me very bitter.

Even now I would appreciate it if she was able to talk to me a little more about it, but more and more I just feel I have to give up on that. I'll never even get a satisfying debriefing from her. Basically, though I'm fairly well detached emotionally from it, I find that I still can't fathom it. How could this woman, my wife whom I loved without reservation, how could she take this kind of posture, to just utterly turn off to the whole thing? I don't know how she could, it hasn't been easy for her, because she's had to deal with her parents, her friends, me. I find a lot of women, particularly married women, are very unsympathetic toward her. I don't know if they're jealous or what, but they're very antagonistic toward her. But like I say, that feeling of helplessness, that feeling that there's absolutely nothing I can do about it, that is the very worst. . . .

Clearly, though it is not yet a well understood syndrome, the most extreme experiences of role reversal carry with them a deep sense of loss, grief, and anger on the part of the abandoned man. Relatively few earnest attempts to analyze and comprehend the experience are yet available. Among those that are, there is a tendency to dismiss role-reversal stress as indicative of nothing more significant than that men resent being made to look like losers or failures, especially in sexual situations.

Even though the increasing sexual self-determination and assertiveness on the part of women was the feature of the women's movement the men we spoke to found most disconcerting, it nevertheless strikes us as overly simplistic to reduce the entire phenomenon of masculine sex-role transition stress to nothing more than the shock of sudden sexual rejection, or the spectre of jealousy that may accompany the abrupt end of an essentially monogamous relationship. For most people, the most complete experience of sexual gratification derives from such a relationship. This inevitable condition of sexual fulfillment always has and probably always will excite some degree of tension and fear of rejection, no matter how casual and commonplace sexual arrangements may become.

In our view, sexual possessiveness, the traditional source of the most extreme types of masculine relationship trauma, offers only a very limited model for understanding the current nature of male sex-role transition pain. Present masculine worry over the changing male role has much wider parameters than the specifically genital. The problem involves the whole spectrum of male-female interactions as well as nearly all of those subtle conventions and social cues that have historically served to define the male role in this society. It is, in short, a diffuse and pervasive cultural phenomenon, not simply a sexual one. As one of our interview subjects explained to us, "Yes, I'm uncomfortable with some of the implications of women's sexual emancipation, but I think the worst shock I ever got in my life was when I went to St. Patrick's one Sunday and there was a woman minister at the pulpit."

Men are discovering that the female pursuit of independence and equality often relegates men to a position customarily associated with women, a position in which they react passively rather than initiate actively, respond rather than propose. This is a position that neither sex respects and one that individuals of both sexes are less and less willing to tolerate for themselves, especially when they are given little or no choice about it.

On the other hand, many women have begun to understand the deep limitations of the traditional female role in this society, have become seriously dissatisfied with themselves and with the level of their aspirations, and are finding that they yearn to make radical, sweeping changes in their lives. As this yearning intensifies, they may also feel constrained by the passive conditioning that has made them hesitate to assert themselves more forcefully in the past. One result of this inherent conflict in the emergent female role is that when a woman does make a bid for greater self-determination, it may appear to be done in an uncompromising, even belligerent fashion. Overcompensating, such a woman behaves in an aggressive rather than self-assured manner. And a few also justify this vehemence by looking for a scapegoat on which to vent their new-found outrage. All too often, this turns out to be the most convenient symbol of putative masculine "privilege," the hapless male.

We spoke briefly with Helen Traner, the ex-wife of the attorney whose traumatic experience of role reversal was presented at the onset of this chapter. Two years after the end of her marriage to Jack, she looks back with some regret at the abruptness of her departure:

> I would do it differently now if I had it to do all over again. I would still do it, but I wouldn't be quite so hard on Jack this time. Walking out like that wasn't really fair, I agree, and I'm still not very

proud of it when I think about it. In the two years since then I've matured a lot psychologically, and when I think about my marriage to Jack, I realize that although I felt like I was suffocating, that wasn't really his fault. I think he loved me enough to let me go, once he realized how much pain I was in, and how much that pain really had nothing to do with him. But it is a chicken-and-egg problem, because when you feel that bad about being trapped in a relationship, you really don't have the psychological strength to unravel it slowly and gently. The best you can do is tear it apart, all at once, sharply. When it gets to that point, it feels like your sanity is at stake, and there's no way you can fault someone who is somewhat clumsy in her attempt to preserve her sense of identity—at least I can't.

But I agree, the burden was on me to say something to Jack, to trust him enough to try to communicate my frustration to him, to let him feel my dissatisfaction, even if it was vague and inarticulate. Unfortunately, I was so good at suppressing my own feelings, at making everything seem to be fine, that there was really no way *I* could know then how unhappy I really was.

I guess I'd also like to make it clear that Jack was blameless. He was not one of those manipulators who undermine their wives by asking them to communicate and then discredit their complaints as being foolish, or self-indulgent, or whatever: You know, men who invite their wives to just go ahead and express themselves and then when she tries to describe how strange she feels, they get panicky and say something like, "There's nothing wrong with you! Don't be silly!" And usually in a tone of voice that manages to imply the exact opposite: "What on *earth* is wrong with you?" Jack wasn't like that. He never put me in double binds like that, and as I've told him since, I sincerely regret having had to make my life change in such a drastic, painful way. But change it I had to, and that I'm not the least bit sorry about.

As we discuss in more detail in Chapter III, the men we spoke to most deeply resented abrupt ultimatums and, in some cases, categorical denunciations, in women's struggles for personal liberation. Unprepared for the desperation that can accompany a woman's longing for greater personal freedom, men found themselves astounded and deeply alienated by the vast, impersonal fury they encountered. To these men, such a woman's exit from a relationship seems to have all the consideration and compassion of a prison break. Surprised and hurt to find themselves cast in the role of guards, they naturally tend to dismiss the entire process as strange and pathological.

Though many men continue to express enthusiasm for the aspirations of any intrinsically democratic movement, the struggle for women's rights has in fact become a highly charged issue for them. They feel threatened by its challenges. Thus a climate of defensiveness about the entire gender issue has developed. A man may automatically interpret a woman's most cautious gesture toward greater autonomy as representing profound dissatisfaction with herself, their relationship, and, most painfully of all, him.

Furthermore, as Dr. Pierre Mornell has recently observed, there is a strong tendency among men, attributable in Dr. Mornell's opinion to a common need for relief from occupational pressures, to react to relationship stress by becoming detached and withdrawn.[2] Unfortunately, this is the sort of reaction that only further frustrates the newly assertive woman, provoking her into more exaggerated demands, which in turn cause further emotional disengagement and intensified avoidance behavior on the part of the man. Compassionate negotiation is precluded as both individuals become frozen into antagonistic positions. Deadlocked, the relationship drifts into a degenerative process. If the polarization continues, the relationship usually ends.

Eventually, if the process of degeneration is allowed to continue unchecked, one partner or the other—and it is now as likely to be the woman as the man—will make the move of issuing an ultimatum, backed up by the threat of separation. If the woman makes the ultimatum, the man is left to feel inadequate, rejected, and self-protective. He is likely to fear that no matter what he does he will never be able to measure up to her escalating demands. For him the culmination of this process is increased pain and helplessness. For her it is painful aggravation of her rage and resentment.

And so it is that men find themselves increasingly taken by surprise, living in a strange new world in which they have suddenly been cast both as villain and victim. Placed in the unfamiliar and uncomfortable position of the reactor, forced to like or lump a woman's changes, their fundamental response is often to feel deeply betrayed. Evidently, they conclude, women believe that their advances can only be won at the cost of men's losses. Upset, disoriented, faced with what appears to be monstrous self-absorption on the part of women, these men personalize a basically abstract, ideological resentment and react by mobilizing their own counteraggressive forces. Secretly blaming themselves for being foolishly gullible and trusting, they may vow never to let it happen again. As one of our interview participants put it:

> To me, the word that keeps coming back is that I felt devastated. I felt devastated. I don't think I've ever felt that bad in my life, as if the bottom had dropped out of it. I had created a whole life with Connie, not just in my mind, but because we had talked about it so much. It was the worst emotional experience I've ever had in my life. I mean, I've had some rocky experiences, like my parents dying, being unemployed, but that was the worst. I'd already gone through a lot more than most people have, and held up pretty well, but I

remember that day at some point I thought, I'm either going to go crazy because of this or I'm going to get very, very sane. You know, I had a choice, essentially. And this took place within a twenty-four-hour time period.

I knew I would either fall apart completely and ruin everything else in my life, everything else I had attained by then, or I would . . . To use a combat analogy, it's like the feeling a guy gets when he's just been shot at and he suddenly realizes someone out there is trying to kill him. He has a choice: Either he can lay down right there and give up, or he can say, "Well, screw it, no matter what happens, I'm going to survive." And I think that was what I was feeling during that critical twenty-four-hour period.

I had wanted to make a commitment to someone, had maybe gone too far out of my way to try to create the situation where I could really make that wholehearted commitment, and then, having really put it on the line, I got my ass shot off. Now I feel like I don't want to go into combat again, in a way. I survived, but I'm a little gun-shy.

Other men, deeply shaken by the sudden loss of a source of comfort and companionship, retreat into even more cynical defensiveness. "You give somebody the opportunity to screw you, and they will, that's what I found out," said one embittered respondent. "It doesn't matter who they are, your best friend, your wife, your kids, it doesn't matter, they'll all do it. It hurts to find out that after giving all this love and good faith to people, they don't bat an eyelash when the chance arises and they turn around and do it to you. From now on, I'm guarding myself against that. Call me impassive, cold, whatever you want, but I'm not going to let anyone get to me like that again."

By and large, the men we talked to do not contest the value of the women's movement. Though their attitudes about feminism, as we discuss in more detail later, are often complex and equivocal, most men accept the movement's compatibility with the egalitarianism that informs this country's most fundamental vision of itself. Furthermore, most men admit that without the example of the women's movement, without the attention that has been focused on both the concrete and attitudinal injustices perpetrated by sexual stereotyping, few, if any of them, would have spontaneously acknowledged their own chauvinism, active or latent, and fewer still would have done anything about it.

We think most men would enthusiastically cooperate in helping to realize the feminist vision of a more equitable society, but they have understandable reservations. Women, after all, have taken the initiative in the gender controversy, and men naturally defer to their place in its vanguard. Furthermore, there are still no clear, consistent cues from women as to what an appropriate, complementary male contribution is in many situations. Indeed, the messages that have been directed at men thus far have been predominantly critical and even punitive. This is why, as William R. Phillips, 1978 president of the Georgia Association of Marriage and Family Counseling observed, "Men have been candy-assed in response to any comment that comes out of the Women's Movement. It's the same posture that Southern Liberal Democrats were in for many years with regard to the civil rights movement."[3]

Finally, it should be remembered that men generally still tend to feel inhibited about overdramatizing or confessing too readily to psychological pain. Raised to be "strong and silent," to equate masculine pride with endurance and toughness, they feel it is undignified for them to react too plaintively to criticism for fear of being considered "crybabies." Unfortunately, even when men do decide to express their fears and doubts, they are then all too often pilloried for being "whiny," "childish," or "dependent," epithets that only reinforce the obsoletely stoic male stereotype.

Many of the women we spoke to admitted that they were tempted to dismiss the entire concept of male sex-role transition stress as nothing more complicated or significant than "the price of change in an oppressive, patriarchal society . . . poetic justice . . . just a case of not being able to take what you dish out." There is assuredly *some* truth in their argument. *Some* degree of masculine role reversal pain is no doubt attributable to nothing more profound or novel than the pangs occasioned by a sudden descent from dominance. Other aspects of current masculine distress are no doubt simply intensifications of the traditional "can't live with 'em, can't live without 'em" ambivalence of men toward women, one that Karen Horney labeled "dread of women."

But in our view there is much more underlying male role reversal pain, and by the same token much more involved in the emergent male orientation toward women, than simple, classic misogyny.

There can be little doubt that male role stress is widespread. As we well know from preparing this book, more and more men are encountering some degree of role transition difficulty in their own lives, and are looking for better ways to understand it and to cope with it. As we worked we could see the entire issue begin to assume more and more prominence in this country's consciousness.

II

Studying and Portraying Men's Reactions to the Women's Movement

RELATIVELY UNHEARD of as a clinical entity in the world of mental health, male sex-role reversal pain is increasingly diagnosed, treated, and discussed in the professional literature. As early as 1976, psychologist and author *(The Hazards of Being Male* and *The New Male)* Herb Goldberg was commenting that:

> The phenomenon of the passive, submissive wife who suddenly and inexplicably turns around and leaves her shocked husband has become very common. Humiliating themselves by going to extremes to win back a woman who had rejected them, many successful, seemingly strong, self-contained, "independent" men have been brought to their knees. Men who appeared to have every-

thing became seriously depressed and suicidal, experienced night terrors, and became physically abusive toward the errant spouse or her boyfriend. They undertook incredibly childish and degrading manipulations in an attempt to win back "their" woman.[1]

In May 1979, in an address entitled "The Effects of the Women's Movement on Men: A Therapist's View" (delivered at the annual meeting of the American Psychiatric Association), Terry S. Stein, M.D., declared that "the women's movement and a new feminist orientation are producing major psychosocial changes in American society."* Dr. Stein went on to comment on the remarkable reticence of men in response to issues raised by women over the last twenty years, at least in terms of their feelings about the implications of these issues for changes in the male role. Noting that "there are virtually no serious studies in this area," Dr. Stein went on to affirm the importance of the issue: "It is essential to arrive at such an understanding of the effects on men of changes in women if long-term changes for both men and women on societal and psychological levels are to be understood and accomplished."

Dr. Stein speculates that men have not articulated their sense of these effects for three closely related reasons:

1. The women's movement has offered so profound a critique of the male role it has led many men "to defend against this attack by belittling or ignoring what women are saying about themselves and about men."

2. Male inexpressiveness: since self-expression is somewhat alien to the traditional male role, men may tend to contain their responses as an attempt to retain some of their traditional power.

3. Simple fear: Men fear the power that women are increasingly advocating, seeking, and attaining. At the same time,

*Dr. Stein is Associate Professor and Director of the Psychotherapy Clinic, Department of Psychiatry, College of Human Medicine and College of Osteopathic Medicine, Michigan State University.

masculine feelings in reaction involve anger and envy, especially of women's relative longevity and their evidently greater capacity for "affective expressiveness and noncompetitive relationships."

Finally, Dr. Stein comments that "every family I have seen in psychotherapy has had to address issues of changes in women during the past several years." The men in these couples, faced with the quest for greater self-determination on the part of their wives, have commonly manifested pathological "guilt, anger, passivity, a wish for revenge, and a variety of other reactions," including, in the extreme, "clinical depression or borderline phenomena in reaction to object loss." Dr. Stein concludes that the effect of these changes in women "on most men is stressful, and on some it may be catastrophic."

The findings of clinicians like Goldberg and Stein have been corroborated and advanced in an especially valuable way by Ellen Halle, M.M.H., a Maryland psychotherapist who is also an instructor in the Sexual Behaviors Consultation Unit of the Department of Psychiatry at the Johns Hopkins Medical Institution in Baltimore.

Reporting first in *Psychiatric News* and later in *Psychiatric Opinion*, Halle describes the "response to separation and divorce, separations initiated in each instance by the wife" of a group of "twenty-six men seen at a mental health clinic at a time of marital turmoil, men who had married in their early twenties, who had themselves been reared in traditional homes and who had traditional expectations of their wives."[2]

Halle defined three groups: "angry grievers," professionally successful men in their late thirties who felt great distress and humiliation at their wives' departure from fifteen-year traditional marriages; "devoted clingers," typically younger, less affluent, passive-dependent or passive-aggressive men whose wives viewed them as dependent and immature; and "detached avoiders," engineers and computer technologists, primarily narcissistic and obsessive, who were "mystified" by their wives' depression and misery but did not complain when their wives left.[3]

In the expanded article appearing in *Psychiatric Opinion*, Halle offered a number of amplifications of her earlier comments. Noting at the outset of the discussion that "much has been written from the viewpoint of women about the pain of separation and divorce, but little from the viewpoint of the 'abandoned' male," Halle then went on to observe that, despite the distinct differences among these three groups of men—angry grievers, devoted clingers, and detached avoiders—"all these men faced the stress of new demands and expectations from their wives, expectations that seemed clearly to have been a consequence of the women's movement of the 1960's and 1970's."

Describing some of the symptoms of the first group, angry grievers, Halle portrayed them as typically being "in a highly agitated state, with copious crying, wringing of hands, and complaints of sleeplessness, inability to function at work, and feelings of depression . . . Several men spoke of the wife's departure as 'like death'; three reported suicidal ideation." According to Halle, "these men were in acute pain, which their wives were unable to acknowledge directly, presumably because of their own massive rage."

In the second group, devoted clingers, Halle states that "in all these men feelings of sadness, loneliness and failure were initially immobilizing. Their wives' departure brought out their passivity and hopelessness. Some husbands remained intensely interested in their wives' new lives, and attempted to prolong the attachment through helpfulness, e.g., babysitting, carpentry, running errands, etc. They had trouble seeing that their helpfulness disguised covert clinging. It was difficult to mobilize their repressed/denied anger and rage and to help them to get in touch with aggressive feelings so that they could function in a more mature, autonomous manner. Fearful of rejection and sexual failure, these men often were reluctant to make new contacts, but when they did, they felt positive and accepted." Many of the wives of this second group of men were "heavily involved in such activities of the women's movement as consciousness-raising groups, self-actualization, couples' labs and assertiveness training . . . When these wives decided to finally end the marriage, almost half preferred to leave their children primarily in care of the husbands, often saying, 'He's a better mother than I am.' The husbands responded eagerly to child-rearing responsibilities."

Halle reiterates in this second article her previous conclusion that "not much is known directly" about the men in her third group, those she labels detached avoiders.

Our own interviews with men tended to underscore the accuracy of many of these clinical reports of role-transition stress in men. At its most intense, the men we spoke to described extremely strong feelings of rejection, betrayal, despair, and above all, helplessness. Preoccupied to the point of obsession, a man experiencing role reversal stress may become restless and agitated. He may pace the floor and feel compelled to go for long aimless drives or walks. He may lose his powers of concentration, causing his performance of occupational or domestic tasks to deteriorate. He may smoke and drink too much. He may overeat, or he may lose his appetite altogether. He will probably suffer from insomnia. He may become intermittently enraged and violent, or he may lapse into depression, becoming in some cases withdrawn to the point of incapacitation.

At less extreme (and much more common) levels, sex-role transition stress manifests itself in primarily verbal ways—as astonishment, ruefulness, sarcasm, self-deprecation, passive-aggressive "endorsements" of the women's movement, immediately followed by "objective" criticisms (the "Yes But" syndrome), or even pointed silence.

It can also include a wide range of psychogenic disorders: headache, backache, stomachache, transient hearing loss, obscure chest pains, tic, stammer, hypertension, and so on. For example:

> I started having a psychosomatic eye problem where I'd wake up in the morning and my eyes would be glued shut. I'd blink my eye and it would

> hurt. My eyes would be sore. Blinking my eye would be painful, and the eye would be red. I went to a number of doctors, but no one could quite figure out what it was. It must have been psychosomatic. I did cry a lot, so it wasn't like I was blocking it out, but it must have had something to do with the intensity of the weeping.

What is particularly disturbing to us about these reports is that the rising incidence of male sex-role transition stress is affecting precisely the same group—adult males—that is already least tolerant of stress in general and is most notably vulnerable to the development of significant stress-related disorders. Taught to achieve, to master, and yet to strive to remain calm, unemotional, and dispassionate, men who experience additional relationship stress have a clearcut tendency to suppress and to internalize their negative responses. In doing so, we believe they court grave physiological repercussions, in the form of ulcers, colitis, emphysema, cirrhosis of the liver, stress-induced arteriosclerosis (men have a 500 percent greater likelihood than women of suffering myocardial infarction), certain forms of cancer, and ultimately, an early grave—some eight to ten years earlier, on the average, than women, and getting earlier all the time.

> The increasing disparity in longevity cannot simplemindedly be attributed to some "natural" female biological superiority. Males have larger heart and lung capacities proportionate to their size and a greater capacity for oxygen in the blood which enables them to recover from exhaustion faster. The oldest authenticated age for a human was achieved by a male. That males are showing these dire longevity statistics must be viewed from the perspective of lifestyles, stresses, physiological habits, emotional repressions, and sociological pressures.[4]

An unfortunate kind of grim negative confirmation of this thesis is now beginning to show up as a rising incidence of stress-connected pathologies among women. As Dr. Harold Roth, Associate Director for Digestive Disease and Nutrition in the National Institute of Arthritis, Metabolism and Digestive Diseases of the National Institute of Health, reports, women are getting more ulcers than ever before. Fifty years ago, according to Dr. Roth, when ulcers were an extremely prominent health problem, only one woman developed ulcers for every twelve men that did. Today that ratio has dropped to one ulcerous woman for every two ulcerous men.[5]

By struggling to maintain an aura of calm, collected control when in fact they feel deeply angry and depressed, men only add to the already extreme stress that their genes and their role conditioning subject them to anyway. When their occupational and lifestyle stress is compounded by emotional turbulence in the one area of their lives—their primary relationships with women—that most men have been led to rely on—almost exclusively—for their sense of affection, acceptance, companionship, and sexual and emotional intimacy, they feel isolated. When this turbulence is exacerbated by attempts to induce in them a sense of individual, personal culpability for the perpetuation of sexist institutions, they are likely to feel beleaguered as well. And when, finally, this process culminates in rejection by women, their reaction is likely to be one of despair.

Without a general cultural acknowledgement of the existence and significance of the problem of male sex-role transition stress, without the development of further ways to describe it and come to terms with it, many men will continue to suffer from it needlessly and to pay a very real and perhaps unnecessary price—both psychologically and physically.

One step that men themselves are going to have to take in this direction for the sake of their own well-being is to become more actively responsive to the issues advanced by the women's movement, to become more aware of how these issues are specifically represented in the women they form important personal attachments to. The tendency of many men either to offer an ingenuous blanket endorsement of the movement or to dismiss anything prefaced with the term "feminist" as being somehow irrelevant to their lives is at the very least a form of poorly disguised condescension, and at the very worst is self-destructively obtuse. In fact, it constitutes abdication of the male right to insist on consideration as an equal partner in *any* movement that advocates gender parity. Most men are learning to accept the fact that they will be regarded as sexist if they presume to speak too glibly about what contemporary women feel and want. It may also be time for them to learn that the burden of creating a more truly reciprocal gender partnership and making it work rests very squarely on their own shoulders. It is the obligation of individual men to articulate, with equal clarity, what they too feel and expect in their relationships with women.

Not only is it arrogant for men to dissociate themselves from the struggle for human liberation embodied by the best of the women's movement, it is also all too often predicated on a naive view of the movement as a monolithic, well integrated, entirely developed set of values and perspectives. This is not the case. Like any other radical revolution in human consciousness, the "women's movement" is highly pluralistic. The term comprises a very large, fluid federation of casual associations, collectives, communes, social action organizations, radical factions, quasi-therapeutic processes, publications, professional networks, businesses, services, corporations, political and sociological philosophies, and, above all, individuals, many of whose convictions are deeply antithetical to those that others most ardently support.

> Like patriarchy itself, the extent and influence of the antipatriarchal women's movement is difficult to grasp. It is not defined by specific organizations, groupings, or factions, though these exist in abundance. It exists in many stages of development throughout the world, at the most local, pragmatic levels, as a network of formal and informal com-

munications, as a growing body of analysis and theory, and as a profound moral, psychic, and philosophic revaluation of what it means to be "human."[6]

—Adrienne Rich

And in a way it is this very pluralism that has contributed most to the difficulty men have had in understanding the true scope and complexity of the women's movement, since it comprehends wildly contradictory attitudes about men. Some of these attitudes, like those expressed by Gloria Steinem and Betty Friedan below, seem inviting and reasonable:

> The goals of the feminist revolution cannot be achieved without a humanization of *both* sex roles. In the deepest sense, revolutionary feminism is a path, the *only* path, to humanism.[7]
>
> —Gloria Steinem

> The movement will have to much more involve men than we thought back then [at its inception]. We should not deny the things that used to define women—the need for security, intimacy.[8]
>
> —Betty Friedan

Others, like this one from *The Women's Room*, by Marilyn French, can only be interpreted as vindictively hostile:

> What is a man, anyway? Everything I see around me in popular culture tells me a man is he who screws and kills. But everything I see around me in life tells me a man is he who makes money. Maybe these two are related, because making money in our world often requires careful avoidance of screwing and killing, so maybe the culture provides the unlived part. I don't claim to know, and I don't even care much. I figure that's their prob-

lem. Women are trying hard these days to get out from under the images that have been imposed on them. The difficulty is there is just enough truth in the images that to repudiate them often involves repudiating also part of what you really are. Maybe men are in the same boat, but I don't think so. I think they rather like their images, find them serviceable. If they don't, it's up to them to change them. I do know that if that is what men are, I'm willing to dispense with them forever, and have children only through parthenogenesis, which would mean I'd have only female children, which would suit me fine. But the other side of the image, the reality, is just as bad. Because if the men I've known haven't much indulged in killing and are no great shakes at screwing and have made money (for the most part) in only moderate amounts, they haven't been anything else either. They're just dull. Maybe that's the price of being on the winning side.

Because the women I know have gotten fucked, literally and figuratively, and they're great.[9]

Finally, it is worth re-emphasizing a point that we all know well at a subliminal level, but which we regularly and understandably tend to overlook. There is enormous momentum built into the fabric of this country's social, political, economic, and legal institutions, a momentum that the compulsive trendiness of American culture leads us to underestimate. The consensus of the men and women we spoke to was that radical changes in the nature of the relationship between the sexes in this country were already well underway, but—and they were equally unequivocal in this second observation—*there are changes that will not take place overnight*. As one man said:

But all that aside, it seems indisputable to me that there has been a division into men going out into the world to earn a living and women staying home to bear and raise kids. And it turned out to limit the kind of life women could live in a way that they now feel is unfair. O.K., so now we know that women don't like these kinds of constraints. So fine, let's change them.

But it's not going to happen overnight. It's a huge problem, and changing it means digging down at the very roots of a lot of patterns that are at the heart of a lot of people's lifestyles. Now in this society we want it all now, and that goes for women too. Well, this isn't going to happen *now*. We're going to have to be patient, and careful, or a lot of people will be badly scarred. So let's change it, but let's change it thoughtfully.

The women we talked to concurred. Said the 56-year-old female director of a political lobbying group in Washington, D.C.,

I regularly meet with women who hold positions of some power in this city. One runs a savings and loan with her husband, another is the CEO of a public relations firm, a third is the executive director of the second largest private foundation in this region—and they all share my concern about moving too fast. The Brave New World charted by some feminists is all well and fine, but we must have the time to make changes carefully or we're not going to be able to help anyone. It isn't enough to have brains and courage, you must have experience too, and in order to get experience, you need time, lots of it.

Our Method

The preparation of *The Male Ordeal* progressed through four more or less sequential stages. First, we studied selections

Studying Men's Reactions to the Women's Movement 51

(listed in the Bibliography) from the voluminous recent literature, both popular and that of specialized professional fields, on such topics as feminism and the women's movement, the family, childrearing, the formation of gender identity in children and its maintenance in adults, and—scant though it still is—the literature on men. Though we can't claim to have covered any of these subjects exhaustively, we believe we became sufficiently acquainted with them to grasp the central issues that inform the current controversy over gender equality.

Second, we spoke informally with literally hundreds of men and women—relatives, friends, friends of friends, colleagues and co-workers, and, in some instances, complete strangers—both married and unmarried, from all parts of the country, from a wide spectrum of lifestyles and socioeconomic backgrounds, from the poor to the very affluent, from the young to the elderly.

Third, we placed this brief ad in a national news publication:

> Author seeks confidential interviews with men aged thirty-five plus who have experienced changes in male role (negative or positive) due to women's movement. Send name, address, phone number and brief description to . . . Privacy assured.

Replies to the ad varied greatly, as the two examples below demonstrate.

> I'm a **-year-old house-husband caring for my **-year-old wife and **** teenage children. We have been married for ** years and for the first ** years we both had busy careers that **** months ago led us to adopting our present lifestyle.
>
> We feel both positive and negative effects of this change but generally have no question that a one-career home is far and away better than a two-career home.
>
> Feel free to contact me if you wish.

Dear Sir:

I am a ******* and ******* living in *******. I married a woman out of college in **** who pursued the ******* profession. We initially began a traditional role arrangement whereby I was the primary breadwinner after graduating from ******* school and my wife's income supplemented the family income. The family, which only consisted of the two of us for a period of about **** years, was highly dependent on my wife during my last two years of ******* school and during my stint in the military service.

After the birth of our first child and the growth and independence of my own *******, the family became dependent on me. My wife continued to work to supplement the family income and to give herself a sense of selfworth and a sense of growth and achievement. When my second child was born I had achieved a greater degree of independence and my wife was feeling a yearning for an independent life of her own. I became much more domesticated in the sense that I was required to fulfill many more nontraditional roles, such as extensive babysitting, child care responsibilities, early morning drives to nursery school, kindergarten, visits to the schools and discussion with teachers, etc. My wife on the other hand became more independent and liberated, seeking the aggrandizement of her "self" and the development of her own personality.

Our marriage was characterized by a series of extramarital affairs engaged in by my wife, some of which began as early as my service years and which were later engaged in when my wife began to enjoy independent vacations away from home.

I can give you greater details, but suffice it to say our marriage has now completely broken up. I have the children during *******, during

******* and *******, and these are the times when my wife who is a ******is off from ******* and going her own happy-go-lucky way. My wife is going through great conflict in her life and our divorce should be concluded any day but notwithstanding the reasonably generous property settlement which we resolved about ******* ago, there is still great antagonism toward me and a kind of latent hostility which never seems to become quite completely dissipated. I never understood it when I lived with her and I cannot completely understand it now.

It is difficult to conduct a ******* activity and at the same time be a good and loving father to my **** little *******. Yet, I feel that I am a more gentle and sensitive parent figure to my ******* than my wife actually is to them. Therefore, the times that I see them are very special to them, and they are constantly asking to see me more and more. On the other hand, I believe that my wife has something significant to offer them and I am convinced that a contested custody battle would be useless. As a result we have the present situation, which is less than satisfactory for me, and I assume that my wife finds it rather hampering to her lifestyle even though she is free of them on ******* and will undoubtedly be free of the children during the *******.

I hope this gives you some insight as to my real life situation and I wish you luck and success in your book.

Very truly yours,
****

Steps two and three had allowed us to compile a pool of candidates for more formal interviewing. In Step four, we contacted each prospective interview subject by phone or in person, explained our project further, and asked whether he or she would consent to be interviewed. Out of forty-three prospective candidates contacted, we were eventually able to obtain the cooperation of and to more extensively interview thirty-one individuals, twenty-seven men and four women.

The ages of interview subjects ranged from twenty-seven to sixty-six, with a median of forty-three. Of the twenty-seven men we spoke with, thirteen were separated or divorced, eleven were married (only one for the second time—the other ten were still in their first marriages), and three had never been married. Of the four women we talked to, two had never been married, one was married at the time of our interview, and one was divorced.

Interviews lasted from a minimum of one-half hour in two cases to a maximum of eight hours in one case. The average interview length was about seventy-five minutes. Twenty-seven of the individuals we talked to volunteered their time for the interview; in three cases we paid subjects a nominal fee as compensation for lost work time.

We had originally intended to concentrate exclusively on men aged thirty-five and over, for reasons which seemed logical at the outset of the project. First, we anticipated that men of this age would be more likely to be married, to have children, to have been raised in a family and cultural environment that inculcated more or less traditional views about male and female sex roles. With careers well underway and family responsibilities to meet, these men would have a heavier economic and psychological investment in the perpetuation of customs, institutions, and values deemed sexist by the women's movement. Thus, we reasoned, men in this age and socioeconomic group would be more likely to manifest clearcut signs of sex-role transition stress. As it happened, and as we discuss in more detail in Chapter III, we could find no support whatsoever for this assumption. Though men of this description were individually as subject to role reversal stress as others, we could find no indication at all that they were any more rigidly or unrepentantly sexist than any other discrete group of men. Furthermore, there was some indication that they were less so, that they were actually *more* reasonable and *more* accommodating *because* of their achievements and experience than other men tended to be. (In fact, the most unabashedly sexist men we spoke to—but did not interview—were between eighteen and twenty-one years old.)

In talking in some depth with this small but, in our opinion, representative group of men, our intentions were threefold. First, we wanted to overcome the inherent biases of our own personal point of view, confirming it where it was validated by the experiences described by the men and women we spoke with, correcting and readjusting it when what we expected to find was refuted by what these individuals told us.

Second, we believe that even though the majority of men in this country may still have only the vaguest intimations of the existence of sex-role transition stress, the gender revolution is in fact influencing virtually every man's life in one way or another. Depicting reversal stress in its fullest, most complete forms, as we have attempted to do here, should alert men to it and should, by familiarizing them with it, help them respond to it more effectively.

Finally, we were just plain curious. Much has been heard in recent years about what women want and why they want it. Very little has been heard from men, not only in specific reaction to women's demands, but also more generally about their view of themselves and their side of the interdependence of the sexes. It no longer suffices for men to take the position that they just want what everyone else wants, to in effect disavow the view that there is anything singular or in any way special about the masculine experience, or about *masculine,* as opposed to *human,* aspirations. At some level, it is true, the project of men and the project of women is the same one, the project of being human, but the pronounced gender re-evaluation of the past few years has made that level an elusive one. We feel, as we elaborate further in Chapter IV, that the best way to re-evoke it depends on the articulation by men of what they find masculinity to mean to them.

Though we feel strongly that any other investigator who did what we have done, who talked to the people we have talked to, and who asked the questions we have asked would arrive at conclusions similar to ours, we do not pretend to statistical validity in *The Male Ordeal*. Our observations should in no way be construed as "scientific." However, we feel with equal conviction that the fact of statistical insignificance in no way renders these comments uninformative, invalid, or meaningless. *The Male Ordeal* is intended to be a discursive, impressionistic presentation of what any informal analysis would disclose through ordinary contacts with ordinary men and women in ordinary circumstances.

It is to the degree that this book clarifies the reader's understanding of the attitudes on the gender controversy of many of the men that he or she knows personally that it should be considered accurate. In this same sense, the process of writing this book offered unexpected insights into our own experiences. Over and over again we found our hunches, suppositions, and vague hypotheses confirmed or even dramatically elevated to a striking new level of intelligibility as we spoke to these people.

However, as valuable as we feel this book to be in illustrating a largely unacknowledged quality of masculine vulnerability, one that deserves a great deal of further exploration, we also want to warn against making categorical generalizations about men or about their expectations of women based on the material presented here. Like women, men do behave in characteristic and surprisingly predictable ways, but, again like women, these cannot ever finally be reduced to one ultimate set of attitudes, traits, or behavior patterns. Like women, men are first and foremost individuals, and they are finally, again like women, unsurpassingly unique beings.

The interview format is a deceptive and elusive one. Subjects have a natural desire to try to discover the unspoken assumptions of the interviewer. In the case of interviews like ours, this desire translated into a tendency to scrutinize us for signs of affirmation or contradiction, then to shape the course of the interview to conform to the former. In this respect, the skill of the interviewer seems to lie in remaining as impassive as possible.

Also, many of the interviews we conducted had a strong exploratory feeling to them. We found in many cases that the men we spoke with, though certainly well aware of the existence of a "women's movement" and familiar in the most general way with its presuppositions, had rarely taken the time to stop to determine their own personal convictions about gender equality. Consequently, they often seemed somewhat surprised to be involved at all in a process that asked them to consider fairly demanding questions about their gender attitudes and their experiences with women, one that required them to give thoughtful responses, and one that showed every sign of taking what they had to say quite seriously.

Structuring and posing our questions became something of a problem too. At first our strategy was to make them deliberately vague and open-ended (e.g., "What do you think of the women's movement?"), hoping to elicit spontaneous responses, unaffected by cues about our expectations or biases contained in the questions themselves. This worked well, after a fashion. We *did* get relatively unpremeditated replies, but we soon discovered that they were also often as vague and ambiguous as our questions (e.g., "Oh, it's a good thing—no reason women should be discriminated against is there?"). Instead of specific details of highly illuminating experiences with role reversal we were getting platitudes.

Furthermore, we also found it difficult, using this open-ended, exploratory approach, to follow a prestructured interview protocol through to its end and cover every topic we wanted to ask about. When a participant would feel stimulated enough to amplify his response to a question because it had triggered a powerful memory or emotion, he (or she) would naturally tend to talk at some length. In the process, he or she usually raised numerous other tangential topics and potentially related issues, all of which usually seemed suddenly much more germane than the next question on our interview schedule. Because we always wanted to pursue any *fresh* line of response that emerged in our conversations, while also wanting to cover certain common topics among many different interview participants, we at first found ourselves somewhat unsure about the best way to proceed.

Finally we developed what seems in retrospect to have been a workable compromise. As well as posing some very broad, nonspecific questions, we also asked a few that were quite a bit more specific and detailed (e.g, "What would your response be in this situation: (a) You ask a new female co-worker, one with the same job title as yours, out to lunch—At the end of the meal you reach for the check and she says, 'Oh no, thank you, I'd prefer to pay for my own'; (b) You hold the door open for a woman and she sharply rebukes you for being a chauvinist; (c) Your wife tells you she wants to attend a weekend seminar for a class she's taking that meets in a different city and will require her to be gone for four days . . ."). There still remained the need to tailor even these questions as specifically as possible to what we were able to learn about each individual respondent's circumstances and experiences, but we were able to obtain more detailed responses.

Listed below are broad statements of all the subjects that we wanted to inquire about. Though not all were fully investigated in each interview, pertinent interview segments and our narrative formulations of the issues that appeared to strike the most responsive chords in our respondents (which did not always correspond neatly to our interests or questions) are presented in Chapter III.

• What is the nature of the male sex-role transition experience? Is there a common pattern to it? What distinguishes the pain of role transition stress from traditional male ambivalence about women? How much of a part in it do sexual fears play? How much reversal pain is perceived rather than actual? How much of it stems from adherence to unrealistic, outmoded expectations of women, and how much is actually attributable to a sudden shift in the relationship's bases, initiated by the woman?

• Why are some men so much more susceptible to sex-role reversal pain than others? Why do some men become dysfunctional to the point of requiring professional intervention, while others, with comparable reversal situations, cope much more self-reliantly? Is this difference a function of personal values, better ego structure, wider friendship networks, alternative social or professional reinforcements, or other factors? Or is it rather a measure of the extent and type of involvement/ dependence on the relationship?

• Are there common attitudes, family backgrounds, or demographic characteristics among men who are more susceptible to reversal stress? Are there corresponding commonalities among their partners? Are there common patterns to the precipitating events in cases of extreme role-transition pain?

• Can a picture of an "at-risk" relationship be developed? An "at-risk" male?

• What kinds of beliefs about masculinity and femininity do these men hold? Do these beliefs in turn imply a specific orientation toward sex roles in a relationship? Is this orientation flexible or rigid?

• What are the attitudes of these men toward traditional monogamous arrangements with women, especially marriage?

• What kinds of ideas about a relationship's value system do these men evince? Have they undergone a definable shift due to reversal experiences? In particular, what place do tenderness, trust, affection, communication, romance, commitment, fidelity, mutual respect play in their perspectives about their relationships with women?

• What does the term "feminism" or "the women's movement" mean to these men? How well-informed and involved in the subject are they? What is the nature of their female partners' understanding of and identification with "feminism"?

• What role do these men consider the women's movement

to have played in their role-reversal experiences? What role do their female partners consider the movement to have played in them?

- Does there seem to be anything intrinsically masculine about reversal pain, aside from the fact that it is currently happening to men?
- What have these men done to cope with their pain? How have they tried to relieve it, to surmount it? Have these methods worked?
- If their relationships have ended, what is the attitude of these men toward future monogamous involvements? If they are actively seeking them, how are they going about it?
- What are the expectations of these men about women in general and their relationships with them? Have these changed due to reversal experiences?
- How do these men feel about the institution of the family?
- If these men are parents, what kinds of values and attitudes about women and relationships with them are they communicating to their children? Is there a conscious attempt on their part to alter traditional gender role typing in their children?
- Have the reversal experiences of these men affected their secondary relationships with women, e.g., work relationships?
- Have these experiences influenced their general sexual orientation or behavior?
- Are these men aware of any discrepancies between the standards they set for themselves and those they expect women to conform to? Do they distinguish between outmoded sexual values and attitudes and those that they feel must be present in any primary sexual partnership?
- Based on what we know of male psychology, male bonding, and what we can learn from these interviews, is a male counterpart to the women's movement a probable or feasible option for men?

Our hope is that *The Male Ordeal* will enable men and women to clarify a necessary distinction between those values that are essential to the success of their genuine partnership and those that are simply the residue of the sexual double standard.

> . . . What each sex knows best has been distorted by a neurotically motivated sealing off from what the other knows best. And this means that to melt what even ordinary men have started in their way to recognize as a killing split—the split between male and female sensibility—males and females, if they are to interact humanly at all, must necessarily join as unequivocally equal collaborators.[10]
> —Dinnerstein

Our conviction is that most men, far from being the insensitive, aloof gender imperialists that they are all too often accused of being, are in fact highly vulnerable individuals who are only now beginning to identify and explore the personal experience that underlies the conventional masculine stereotype. Depriving them of the sense of alliance with women that is needed to examine this experience fully and confidently would indeed be unfortunate, and would only prolong the sense of gender divisiveness that now pervades this culture. More than anything else, the distress of the estranged male and his difficulty in coping with sex-role transition is based on his fear of the threat of absolute repudiation, rejection, and abandonment by the women he loves.

Understanding the genuine vulnerability of men to women is a powerful tool for personal and cultural change. But it must be used carefully and compassionately or it will only contribute to further polarization between the sexes, further social fragmentation, and thus more pain for all of us. It must be explored in conjunction with a strong affirmation of gender partnership, with an abiding appreciation for the interdependence of men and women, and for the responsibility of each sex to include the other in its quest for selfhood.

III

Men Respond: The Interviews

THIS SECTION presents the highlights of the thoughts and feelings expressed in our formal interviews. We begin with a typical story, told by Harold Varrick, the forty-three-year-old assistant superintendent quoted in the first chapter. His interview captured perfectly all the major themes that we found running throughout our conversations with these men.

Following Varrick's interview, we present ten major issues that emerged from these conversations and discuss each one in some detail, using additional extracts from other interviews. In brief, we found that the men we talked to tended to be: (1) cautiously supportive of the women's movement, but concerned about its potential to become repressive, (2) most unequivocally opposed to economic discrimination against women while at the same time most perplexed by their sexual emancipation, (3) uninterested in "men's liberation" as a formal movement, (4) strongly convinced of the value of the distinction between masculinity and femininity, (5) strikingly monogamous, (6) very supportive of the conventional nuclear family, especially for the sake of childrearing, (7) convinced of children's need for parental figures of both sexes, (8) divided over the issue of two-career families, (9) not at all worried about the perpetuation of negative sex-role stereotyping in future generations in either boys or girls, and (10) very much aware of and disturbed by the special propensity of some men to suffer extreme emotional distress upon the termination of primary sexual relationships.

Harold Varrick's Story

When I think of the quote "the women's movement," it makes me immediately think of the black movement, the sixties. During most of the sixties I worked for a redevelopment agency in Boston. A large part of my job was to manage a number of legal projects in black neighborhoods. I went through that whole experience of being the only white person in a black neighborhood. So in that process I learned that I have to admit that I'm definitely not black, just like now I have to admit I'm definitely not female. I had to learn not to overidentify with the other role and that I'm still, you know, the white person in the black neighborhood, and tolerate the role that some blacks will give you, in a poor neighborhood, to learn to accept subtle kinds of reverse racism. And then be comfortable with it—don't try too hard to overcompensate by being too liberal. And now with the women's movement, I feel like I'm in a second wave of attack. The women's movement came in on the heels of the black movement, and I also said to the women's movement, "You're right. There should be equal pay, there should be equal jobs, men should change diapers . . . you cannot argue intellectually against any of those precepts."

Now I'm at the point where I say, yes, that is all right and correct. But I am not a woman. And I'm not going to overidentify as I have with the women's movement and march and demonstrate with them. I'm not going to put myself on the cutting edge of it in terms of losing my identity as a male. But I am going to support it, as a male.

I don't quite know what that means yet, to support it as a male. I've thought a lot about it, though, because in the black movement I was in discussion groups in church, becoming more sensitized to blacks, becoming more deeply involved in the psychology of the whole thing. In the women's movement, my younger sister has had to fight to become a firefighter, and I've been through the whole thing with her, very much in support of her. In fact I've been to innumerable meetings with her, and have spoken on her behalf and in behalf of other women who are trying to get into public employment, particularly minority women. So I feel I have been very much in support of the women's movement so far, as a male.

And I've never had any qualms about my wife—now she's my ex-wife, of course—working. I mean, I can't understand how some men can say, "My wife will never work." If she works it just takes the pressure off me in terms of her being unhappy, lonely, isolated, and it helps pay bills. So, you know, why shouldn't she? I'm frankly very proud of the fact that I'm one of the more enlightened men I know in terms of the women's movement. My consciousness has been raised, first by the black movement, now by the women's movement.

But I'm being victimized in this situation too, in some ways a damn sight worse than she is. Because in all these things I feel like I'm being manipulated. All these things are happening to me and because my consciousness is somewhat raised, I can't insulate myself. I can't say, "Goddam it, these gals are all just crazy." I can't dismiss it. So I'm vulnerable. I feel I have become a victim *because* my consciousness is raised, whereas if I was an autocratic old tyrant and was not at all self-conscious, if that was my true makeup and I was authentically that, then I could wander through these sociological minefields, just dumb enough not to worry about it, and get through to the other side unscathed . . .

My major criticism is that the women's movement doesn't have a sense of humor. The black movement did. It had Dick Gregory, Bill Cosby and it sure as hell has had and still has Richard Pryor. A sense of humor and a certain amount of objectivity. And my criticism of the women's movement is that it doesn't have that . . .

Most men I know are not really open to dealing with the women's movement. I'm thinking particularly of in a work situation, where a woman's trying to get a particular job and all they can see are the lawsuits that are threatened, the breakdown of the system, and all that. And I find that my colleagues will promote women under threat, whereas I have an extremely clear conscience in that respect. You know, I know I'm not biased. I tell a woman who tries to pressure me, "You're not going to blackmail me because I have a good record." I'm clear in my own head on this, I'll stand firm, and so I'm not ever made the target of threats or lawsuits.

On the other hand, it is nevertheless quite true that women who want to advance are having to take an antagonistic stand. In some ways it's good strategy on their part. You just have to knock over the chairs in a room to get their attention at first . . . But it's not a consistent attitude in women. For example, you'd be astonished how many women whom I interview for jobs, very liberated women, tell me that they will not work for a woman. If a man were to say that they'd shoot him, but I run across a lot of women who apply for work and say, "I don't want to work for a woman." I guess because they feel that women are more critical of other women.

I always say to them, "What about solidarity? This is really weird." And then they say, "Yes, I know it's weird. I want to get promoted and get good jobs, but I don't want to work for a woman." I've heard that from at least four women that I've dealt with professionally in the last six months. Their image is of the old battleaxe who's in charge of the typist pool, who's hard as nails, who, you know, drives them all too hard, bitches at them constantly, treats them like slaves.

Maybe it's because they sense that that battleaxe is going to be like the black—that's my analogy—who finally makes it in the business world, in the white business world, who says, O.K. now in order to fit in I've got to make a point of being fair, I'm different but I'm not going to promote another black just because he's black, you know, gets real hardnosed and says I'm not typical, and the woman supervisor does the same thing. In other words, you always deny your fellows, once you make it to a certain rung on the achievement ladder, you have to have those qualities to get into the system, to integrate into it . . . To me it seems to imply that what liberation is really all about is kind of like getting your share of the pie. And once you know you're squarely in the mainstream, you're willing to conform real quick in order to make sure the benefits come your way . . . often you're co-opted by the system.

However, I must say that the women I see professionally in the last two years are just being who they are. They're not necessarily conforming to any kind of predetermined idea of how to behave or act in order to get ahead. They're a lot more authentic, they're just being who they are, and, you know, if you don't like the way they dress, or something else about them, tough . . .

I do think women have been oppressed. For example, when I look through history books and I read about the suffrage movement, it's unbelievable to me that it happened so recently, that women couldn't vote until early in this century . . .

Actually the Chair of our Board is a woman. She's about fifty-six years old, very dynamic, but she's also been a homemaker all her life. And in her speech that she gives to these women's groups she's always getting invited to she says, "You're going to have to stop thinking of yourselves as a group. I got where I am as an individual. You can do it too. You know, all this business about prejudice and discrimination, well, while it's always been there, it's up to each one of us to overcome it for herself."

That's an effective approach. I think it's mostly middle-aged women who have more of a tendency to take the group approach. Younger women—by younger I mean under forty, say twenty-five to forty years old—have less of that tendency, in my experience. The very youngest, under twenty-five, I don't know what their relationship to the women's group is. But that middle group, twenty-five to forty years old—you read in the newspapers about them driving trucks, working on power lines for the phone company, becoming police officers, and all that—well in the interviews that I do with that kind of woman, every one of them tells me, "I am not a feminist. I identify with the women's movement, and I consider myself liberated, but I am *not* a feminist." They all make it a point to declare that they are individuals and that they're going after nontraditional jobs on their own.

My theory is that in every woman's breast there beats a desire to be a whole person. And it's been like that forever. Everyone has that aspiration to be a whole, unified, integrated human being. And out of all these aspirations, we've recently had something like a spontaneous combustion, starting with the black movement. Rather than the movement affecting individuals, I think the individuals created the movement. And then they started talking to each other, and then we had a movement. Rather than having it come down from the top, I think it comes up from the bottom. I think these human rights movements are genuine grassroots movements.

In a way, this is our truest legacy of democracy. A century ago you had all these blacks trying to escape from the plantations because they didn't have their personhood, their dignity as human beings, and so they started taking the railroad north. And to me it's the same kind of mentality in the women's movement—you have all these women trying to get on the underground railroad and get out of there. It's not as though someone starts out by saying, "O.K., now we're going to have an underground railroad . . ."

It's harder for me, when I get to my own situation, to be quite so objective and intellectual. My wife and I are both college graduates. We got married at age twenty-seven and waited three years to have children. So we could have time together. It's become a very common pattern for couples now. Lois worked for the first three years and took two years off to have children. Then she went back to work.

At the time we split up, a year ago, she told me a story. "Six months ago," she said, "I was standing in the laundry room one day sorting clothes, and I asked myself, 'Do I want to be doing this forever?'" And then she looked at me and said, "I really don't want to be married. It's not you personally, necessarily. But I just don't want to be married to anybody right now. I was with my father, and after that I was with my husband, and I want to know what it's like to be on my own."

My reply was, "Well, gee, maybe we haven't given you enough freedom within the marriage. Maybe it's so ingrained in me, so much a part of me to expect certain things that we just haven't looked at it from the right perspective yet, maybe I don't realize what kinds of things are keeping you back, or . . .

And she looked at me again and said, "No, Hal, it's not you. It's just that I don't want to be married anymore. I want to be my own legal entity."

And I said, "Well, there's only one thing to do, only one way for you to become your own legal entity, and I can't help you with that, you know, you have to divorce me to become your own legal entity."

But to me, that was the worst, the low point, when she said that. Because everything else, anything within the marriage, you can try to work it out. "Well, if we did this differently, if I came home on time, you know, if I took more time with the kids, if you got away more times during the year on your own." You can do all those things, but when someone says, "Look, I want to be my own legal entity," there's nothing you can do, but say, "Oh." It's an ultimatum, no matter how gently it's put, and you feel absolutely helpless.

She said, "The last year or two I've had this feeling," and actually she'd mentioned it to me once before. At that time I had said, "You can't do that, what are you talking about, it's absurd." Then she didn't mention it for a while. But this time, before she said anything, I felt it. I felt anxious but didn't know what it was, and I asked her, "What's wrong? What is it? I feel something."

She said, "You remember what I talked about to you before? I have the same feelings. I don't want to be married anymore." And then she also said, "And I want to know other men." That really killed me. She explained when she says "knowing" she isn't just talking sexually. She's talking about friendship, openness, sharing, all those things that a marital situation tends to inhibit and preclude.

And you know, I heard what she said, and I believe she feels that way, but I don't have any kind of corresponding feeling on my part. I mean, I don't want to know a lot of women, or anything like that. I want to stay married. To her. . . .

I know she's aware of the women's movement and that she definitely feels she's been enlightened by it. I would have to say it's affected her, yes.

I think I understand it. I mean, I feel like it's been important to me to feel like I'm self-sufficient in some way, psychologically. So I can kind of identify with it, in a way. But to assert it in the middle of a commitment like marriage and a family, to the point of refusing to deal with any kind of counseling, to just absolutely reject any kind of invitation to talk about it, to work through it, to just say, "This is it," and deliver an ultimatum that leaves me with a lot of very difficult, turbulent, painful feelings completely unresolved, that's very hostile and aggressive, to say the least. Sometimes I think it's crazy.

It's how people characterize the seventies, you know, "The Me Generation." But it's more than that. All I can say is that for her it's a gut-level drive, like nothing can get in her way, nothing can stop her. It's like a survival drive. It's life and death. Like she's saying "I'll die, I'll die, I'll actually physically die," if she has to stay in the marriage. She'll somehow vanish, be annihilated.

I don't think men are really quite aware, generally, that there is this kind of desperate strength of determination going on in many, many women. They don't understand the power of what is really going on, that women are feeling smothered and that they are not going to let anything get in their way if they want to break out.

I know I was in disbelief, and I know that lots of men I know are getting the shock of their lives, every day, from their wives . . .

Everything you can come up with as a man, every reason for you to stay together, the woman will reject. My wife said, "I think my children should know that I have relationships with several men. I think that they have to learn to live in this world as it is, and this is my authentic self, my genuine behavior." Hearing that, it's now the man who finds himself saying, "My God! Is that how I want to raise my kids?" He's reactive once more. I had no choice, I had to say, "Well, as far as I know, you're a good mother, so if that's the value you hold, then there's no doubt that they're going to be influenced by it." A man can no longer, like men of our father's and grandfather's generations, just say, "My children are going to be raised X, Y, and Z." That's just gone. Men don't know what they can do or can't do anymore . . .

I really don't know what to do with all this. I'm totally helpless. I feel like I'm being totally reactive to other people's situations. First the black situation, then the women's movement. And so what's my option?

I'm still in a reactive mode. I'm always reacting,

responding to other people's demands, never really able to initiate my own. When she says "I don't want to be married," I have to say, "O.K., we'll get divorced," and because of that I now have to learn a whole new lifestyle, a whole new repertoire of what it means to live as a single individual . . . not only that, but also as a single parent. This isn't happening to me because I set out, like she did, to actively change things, to become single because I wanted to. It's someone else's desire to be single again that is *forcing* me to stop what I was doing, being married, and start doing something completely different now, something I like less.

It makes me wonder where men are going. It's one thing after another. I asked her once, I said, "What's it going to be after the women's movement, what's the next wave that's going to hit us?" And she said, "The children's movement." And I'm afraid she's right. Those teenagers are going to murder us. And they're going to be right. We won't be able to deny them. Just like women and blacks are right.

But it worries me about men because they always wind up identified with the status quo, and then they just have to sit there and take it while everyone else gets to break away, rebelling safely because they know that men are stuck once again holding the bag, keeping society intact and its institutions functioning. Men just get lost, they get submerged, they can only react to things. And they also get duped, caught up in their careers, achievement, power, success, and all that so there's enough stability so that dissatisfied factions can express their antagonisms. Men are stuck with the responsibilities that everyone else finds so repressive and fascist and they have to just sit there and take it. They're dying earlier and earlier, and they're rushing around like crazy trying to keep it all together, to keep going, trying hard to make it, to achieve, to be successful, and it just turns to ashes in their hands . . .

Now, let's take the post-separation phase, because a lot of the difficulty with liberation is driven home to me there: Children.

Now we've been physically separated for three months. But once she told me that she didn't want to be married anymore, we didn't fool around. Three months later we signed the custody papers. We did it immediately because I didn't want the whole thing to start wavering and waffling and have it destroy my life. I said, "If that's the way it is, if it's really that inevitable, then the quick, clean separation is best." I've seen guys, friends of mine, torn apart for years in these situations. So I said, that's not me, I'm not going to grieve about this thing forever, it'll eat me up if I do, I'll die. So her need to escape, on a survival level, triggered a kind of ruthlessness in me, on a similar level of emotional survival. I think that's the only way it can go.

And we did that part of it very well. One of the things I did was I said I wanted joint custody. See, that's the male response: O.K., if this is going to become a free-for-all then I want to hang onto the thing that I really care for in this marriage, the children, and I'll fight you for it if I have to. You know, guys my age and younger are often in the delivery room when the kids are born and it gives you a whole different relationship with them, a totally different role than our fathers and grandfathers had. Now in some states joint custody is a reality, though lawyers don't like it, it seems ambiguous to them. I felt that that was the first and best alternative to be considered, at least from my perspective on the situation. So I pulled together some information on it, articles, books, and so on, and gave them to Lois to read, and she did and she agreed that joint custody would be okay.

However, and this is an important point, the law still has a long way to go. Even though it's a joint custody situation, and *she* initiated and filed for divorce, I'm still winding up stuck with the tab. I have to pay her as though she had sole custody. It's blatantly unfair, but the courts have these charts they go by that say if you earn X dollars, you pay her Y dollars, and that's that.

So I'm still bound by that whole system, that whole point of view, even though in the joint custody relationship I have the kids forty to forty-five percent of the time. Plus I have all the expenses of two households. I've bought beds, dressers, furniture, and created rooms for the kids in my place. They identify with both houses. They're still in the same school district and have the same friends, so their lives haven't been too disrupted, but sociologically and legally, the whole approach to marriage and childrearing is in transition and I've been caught in the crunch, with all the economic burdens, including not only child support but spousal support, which is something I didn't offer and do not feel I should be paying.

Again, here's another situation where the male is victimized and I have strong feelings about that. When was the last time you heard a feminist arguing that if women want to be equal they will have to stop taking spousal support when they initiate a divorce? I mean it's a blatant ripoff, especially when my wife's earning potential is exactly the same as mine. She can make just as much, perhaps more money than I can. Nothing's stopping her. The victimization of the male is that even though it's a no-fault divorce I still legally wind up with the responsibility for spousal support, which is the same thing as alimony, though it has a different name. It's alimony. *I'm* the one who should be getting spousal support! The chart the courts use says you pay alimony for a number of years equal to half the years you were married. We were married fourteen years, so legally I would have been obliged to pay Lois spousal support for seven years, but she said she only wanted it for three. And so I'm paying her $750 every month, $450 for child support, $300 for spousal support. Spousal support is deductible. When it stops after three years, I'll raise the child support by $50-$100 to make up for inflation. She nets about $1200 from her job, so she has a monthly income of $1950, while I'm having to live on about $800. This whole situation makes me extremely angry. I'm being penalized through having to live in an entirely different way than is appropriate for me now, all because she did not want to stay married anymore, but was willing to take some of the benefits of having been married. And she doesn't even have the children full-time. I'm victimized and I can't do a thing about it. I sure can't have my day in court, because the system the courts use to be "fair" is what put me in this mess in the first place. My lawyer, you should hear my lawyer, who by the way happens to be a woman. She says, "Look, this is the way it is for the time being. I think you're crazy to ask for joint custody. Joint custody is wrong, it never works, you'll never get the judge to go for it, and besides, your wife's going to have the money, why not let her take care of the kids? How are you going to be able to make rational decisions about the kids when you can't even stay married? Someone has to be in charge of the kids' lives. How are you going to handle that? And how am I going to deal with it as a lawyer?"

And I said, "What do you mean someone has to be in charge? We split the responsibility for raising the kids now, why can't it work the same way when we're apart? There are some areas with the kids' lives that I don't care about, I don't get involved in, they're her areas. Then on other matters I take a very strong interest, so we manage to cover all the bases pretty well. It's going to be the same kind of arrangement, and I think we can handle it without any problems."

And that's how it actually works with a lot of divorced couples. They have some kind of complementary roles with their kids. She feels that X is her area of responsibility, so she takes charge of that. Maybe it's how they're doing in school, how they're dealing with their teachers. He has other areas, like helping them with their homework, or taking them out to see the relatives, or whatever—anyway they usually find that things like that sort themselves out naturally, and that's how it works in our case.

But I go to teacher conferences a lot more now. Before I'd drop in from my office or I'd skip it. I want to know their teachers and I want their teachers to know me. I have more of that kind of a role now, so I need to know what the teacher says about them for myself. . . .

One thing I think we did very well, handled very well was the way we told the kids about the divorce. Lois had the view to begin with that we should just tell them how we felt, just kind of blurt it out. I didn't agree. I said, "Oh, no, there must be someone who's been through this before and there must be a way to handle it that's easier than others, that's less traumatic for them, anyway. I want to read something about it first." So I did, I looked around, found some things that I thought were pretty good, though I can't remember exactly what they were at the moment, one was a handbook on divorce written by a doctor, covering all sorts of situations that came up with children. I gave it to Lois to read, and basically the point it made was to tell the children together. Have them together, and be sure you and your wife are together, and make sure you emphasize the fact that it's not their fault, that they didn't create the problem, that it's Mom and Dad who have the problem, and so on. Otherwise, they tend to blame themselves, and that causes all kinds of difficulties later. My fear was that we would get everyone together, and we would tell them, and then my eleven-year-old would go, "Oh," and that would be it. There'd be no other reaction from him, just that sickening "Oh." And I thought the younger one just wouldn't understand it at all, would just be bewildered by it or something.

So for a few days after we had both been through that book and made our minds up how to tell the kids, there was a lot of wavering around, back and forth, not quite knowing whether the time was right or not. You know, we'd say, "Should it be today?" and I kept saying, "No, no, I'm not quite ready yet, I haven't worked it out yet, let's wait a little longer." I wanted to prepare and my wife just wanted to tell them what she felt on the spot, just dump it on them.

So finally we got it together and the four of us sat down. Again, I feel a little bitter about a couple of things here. Even though I was the one who was being divorced, Lois just clammed up. She wasn't going to say anything at all when push came to shove and the children were sitting there waiting, knowing something important was going to happen, and feeling worried. I had to start the session, because Lois didn't want to do any of the dirty work. So I said, "You know Mom and Dad love you very much, but we're going to get separated and we'll live in different places. We love you both. It's not your fault," and so on. It really went well. I did it excellently. But Lois didn't say anything at all. I had to do it.

Then all of us started crying, which was what I really wanted to have happen, you know, because the reality of what was happening was so painful, and I wanted it to be understood and gotten out there, opened up, so we could all get through it. It was painful, and we all held each other, and I just felt like there could be no hesitating on our parts then, me or Lois, it just couldn't happen that we'd start sending our kids double messages. So they wouldn't start to wonder about it and ask, "When are you going to get back together?" and all those other anxiety questions, because they would know that that was that, we weren't waffling. I think today they have no anxiety about the situation because we made it a point to never waver, to never let it all seem ambiguous. People comment on how well our kids seem to have adjusted to the situation.

I feel very strongly that that is the way it needs to be done. Once a couple has made its decision to be apart, to split up, they should stay apart, particularly for occasions like Christmas and New Year's that are so reminiscent of families. Unfortunately, 99 percent of the divorced couples I know don't handle it that way. They keep getting back together on those kinds of occasions and I think they just make it harder on themselves and on their kids. They pull themselves apart emotionally. I know I can't deal with it. . . .

It's been about a year now since we split up, and I think it's going very well with the kids. I think they're handling it very well. Everyone comments on it, which is reassuring to me.

When we were first going through this, everyone said, "Ah, it won't work out, you guys are too idealistic. You're doing it well now, but it's going to break down, you're going to start fighting." But we haven't fought over anything, even the property settlement. I always said, "No, it won't break down. We won't have to start fighting about it." Now it's a fact, the divorce is a fact, and it's working out well. No one hates anyone else. The in-laws and the grandparents are all still friendly. The kids go to the same school they've gone to for years, have the same friends, see the same people, live in more or less the same neighborhoods. They bring their friends over to my house or my wife's equally.

Within forty-five minutes after we had told them we were splitting up they started asking questions, like "Will we have the same friends? Will we go to the same school?" Questions about things that affect them and their lives, which I think is great because it's their survival that's involved too. I mean, they're saying, "O.K., you guys may have a problem but I need to know what it means about my life." So I really feel that in the long run, it's going to continue to be like that because there isn't any threat to them, not that I can see. . . .

I still have a problem with the separation, though. I find myself waking up in a cold sweat, thinking, "How did this happen to me? What's this really all about?" That kind of thing.

I called my wife up about two weeks ago, and I asked her, very calmly, very rationally, I said, "Do you have a few minutes?" Because I haven't really ever had a chance to talk to her about our relationship with the kids, about what it means in terms of our relationship with each other that we're still equally involved with our kids. So I said, "Now tell me again why you wanted to do this?" I wasn't trying to put her on the spot, or anything like that, I just wanted to hear it again, because when something like this hits you more or less out of the blue you have trouble taking it in, understanding it, believing it, so you have to hear it over and over again to make it become real to you.

I know other men feel this way too. Something hits you, it's a shock, and it's hard to grasp it, really believe it's really real. You keep forgetting the most painful parts. All you want is to have them said to you over again, because you can't quite believe they're real, you can't believe they're happening. It gets unreal very quickly. It's just that hearing it makes it more real.

Anyway, when I called and asked if she had a minute, and why she had wanted to do this, she said, "Oh come on, you know why."

And I said, "No, I'm very calm, I'm not emotionally distressed or anything like that, but I just want to have an understanding of those words, those feelings that you have again."

And she said, "All right, do you want the long or the short answer?"

I said, "Whatever you have, I want it."

She said, "Well, if you remember, I'm doing this because I really want to live on my own. I want to know what it's like to be on my own, to be a single person, because I've never had a chance to find that out."

And I said, "O.K." And then I couldn't help it, I heard myself saying, "Look—." I went through the same argument as before, "Look, couldn't that have been done within the context of the relationship? I mean, couldn't you have found out about your strengths and weaknesses and your special qualities without getting a divorce?"

She said, "And I want to know other men. I know that's painful for you to hear, and it's painful for me to say it, but there it is." Then it hit me again. I said, "Oh, yeah, I'd forgotten that." And she said, "That's really it." And I said, "O.K., thank you," and I hung up. It was weird, because I felt horrified and emotionless at the same time. It was awful to hear, but I didn't have any strong reaction to it. It was more like internally I was saying, "Aha!" and the pieces dropped into place again. It was—it made sense, psychologically, even though it was terrible. . . .

I went through a terrible crisis last week, after that call. It was the worst week I've had so far with this thing, but I got through it and I'm on a real high about my life now that I'm over the worst. I found out that Lois was going out with someone I know, a man I know quite well, someone who's married. When I found that out, I just got raging mad at both of them, at her and at him. And I got in contact with him and told him, "You betrayed a trust, you and I were friends and now you're seeing my wife." I came on very strong, threatened him, told him I understand how people could commit crimes of passion, all that. They both thought I was nuts. I sounded like a madman. But to his credit, he came over to my place and we talked and I was able to get my rage out and he was able to listen to how I felt.

So when I felt like I'd said what I had to say, I told him, "O.K., now you tell me what you're about here, how you feel." And he said, "Hal, I'm a little afraid to, I feel like you'll just go nuts again, I don't want to provoke you, make it worse for you."

So I told him, "No, no, it's O.K. now. I'm

alright, I'm over it, just tell me how you feel about her and about this situation. I just want to hear about it now."

And then he started opening up more and more, because we're friends, he isn't a stranger, and he said, "Hal, I know this is hard for you to believe but my feelings about Lois are as strong as yours were, maybe more, I really care for her."

Ironically, when he said that, instead of feeling outraged again, I found myself thinking, you poor dear man. He's exactly where I used to be, but he doesn't know this woman. She wants to be free and if he starts to box her in, she'll sock him in the jaw. I know her. I said to myself, he has the problem now. And an amazing thing happened. As all this was happening, all this was going through my head, I found myself emotionally letting go of her, letting her go for good. I said to myself—it was a definite sensation, like a chill running down your back—I said, it's not only that she wants to divorce me, it's also now that I'm one-hundred percent certain that I don't want to be married to her either. I know what I want in a marriage—mutuality. I'll never chase any woman again and go through this. Either it's mutual, we both want it, and we both know we both want it equally, or it isn't going to happen. So I feel great. It's over for me now. My crisis is definitely over.

But there are aspects of it that still make me sad. Even in my casual relationships with women, I get more of that kind of mutuality from relative strangers than I felt we got in our marriage. And I didn't know that until I stepped out of the situation. You see possibilities that you didn't recognize before. I mean there're possibilities for a man too, in the women's movement.

But again, I'm doing all these "wonderful,"

"new," "liberated" things, all this self-education on my part, my second adolescence so to speak, making male as well as female friends, all this I'm doing because someone else, my ex-wife in this case, *made* me. Because of a fairly traumatic thing, a divorce. If she could overhear this conversation, she would say, "Well, look what I did for you," and that's not entirely inappropriate. But it's also true, I would say back to her, "Yeah, but damn it, I've been manipulated again. Once more I have to react, to become excellent in a whole new lifestyle. I have to learn a whole bunch of new social skills, and so on, how to meet people, all that, not because I *chose* to, but because someone else *forced* me into it, because somebody put me on the spot, selfishly, not altruistically, not because they loved me and wanted me to change, but because they decided they wanted to change themselves and they were so closely wrapped up in my life that now, whether I like it or not, I've got to change too. . . .

I dated within two months after we separated, and I'm a guy who's never felt all that comfortable around women I don't know very well. It really is like a second adolescence for me, and it's difficult. In part because for all their talk about being liberated, women still wait for the man to make the first move, even when there is a mutual attraction that is obvious to both of them. So I'm struggling with the whole dating syndrome. How do you make contacts with women? How do you reenter the dating mainstream? All that.

I decided I didn't want to date anyone under thirty, because I tend to find that they don't have their parental ambivalences worked out and those tend to get mixed up with whatever's going on between us. I just don't want to have to deal with a twenty-seven-year-old woman who's unconsciously relating to me as though I were her father. And I decided I didn't want to date anybody at work because that's so tacky. It always struck me as desperate and somewhat unimaginative that men wind up going out with their secretaries and all that. There should be enough other women for me to meet. And I definitely don't want to go bar hopping, that's not my style. And I don't want to date anyone in my church. But then, who does that leave? That pretty much covers my whole life. That leaves no one. That leaves outer space.

So I broke my rule the first time I went out with someone. She was a psychologist, a consultant at work, but it wasn't someone I work with daily. I just knew I had very strong emotions toward her, was very attracted to her, and that they were stronger than was really appropriate to our work situation, so I acted on them. We went out, I guess it was maybe three times.

And I found myself writing to her and expressing really strong feelings for her, and so on. Not saying, I love you, I want to live with you, but just telling her how much she moved me, and wanting to hold her, and so on. But it got to the point where she said, "Well, you know, I like you a lot, but I think you're coming on a little strong at this point." So we cooled it off.

Then I called a woman whom I'd seen around my new place and said, "Look, this is Harold Varrick upstairs. I may never run into you again, so let's get together for a few minutes and talk and see if we might like to go out together." Well we did, but—and this is incredible to me, to find this in the middle of the 1980's—she turned out to be a very religious person who absolutely did not want to go out with a divorced man. That amazed me.

Then just last week I went out with a woman I knew when I was younger who lives near here and who works in a bank downtown, is an assistant manager I guess. And with her I said to myself, after these other experiences, and after having read a lot, I said, just go out and have a good time with her, don't make a pass, don't try to make it physical too quickly. If it comes to that stage, that's a bonus, but don't push it.

And that's what I did. I did exactly that. And it worked. I was relaxed, and just enjoyed her company, and she gave me a goodnight kiss, at her own initiative. And I did something else a little different with her. With the others, I had felt a little clingy, like, gee, I wonder if I'm ever going to see this woman again. But with her I just said, "Give me a call." And she responded. She said, "Yeah, I will give you a call." So rather than me being the one to have to take on the job of carrying the whole thing forward, having to say, "I'll call you. I really want to see you again. When can we see each other?" at the end of the date, I just let her take it on, I stayed out of that trap. I said to myself, "I'll be damned if I'm going to get caught in this again, always being the initiator and then having to just take the crap when everything falls apart and all I can do is react. I'm not going to get nailed again."

After those first few dating experiences, I found I was better able to say, you know, "It's going to be alright, I am going to meet women." Now the big thing in my mind is, relax. Hold back. And, "I'll be goddamned if I'm going to be the one always doing the chasing." Because the woman I married I chased hard, I really worked at it, and I really struggled to set it up, then I got it and lost. Now my big word is mutuality, mutuality of relationship. She's got to want me at least as much, if not more, as I want her, and she's got to let me know that in her actions. I don't know if my bank friend will ever call me again, but I think she will. At least I'm not stuck with the whole responsibility for the thing on my shoulders, and that's a big relief.

Our Fridays

• *These men definitely support the women's movement, but their support is cautious, heavily qualified, and somewhat uninformed.*

"It's a good thing, but . . ." was the immediate response of almost every man we talked to when we solicited his opinion about feminism and the women's movement. "In the long run, it will be men who really benefit from it," declared more than one of our respondents. One man, a fifty-year-old executive in a large utility company in the Pacific Northwest, put it like this:

> I think the feminist movement is a good one, given the changes that have been taking place in our society for at least the last fifty years, maybe longer, maybe ever since the Industrial Revolution . . . There's no question, as far as anyone can tell from the archaeological and historical records that we have, that this has always been a culture in which the male was dominant, was expected to be dominant, for that matter. I mean, you can't argue the fact that men have always been at the center of myth, religion, politics, whatever. Even the family . . . even raising kids, which everyone is always saying was traditionally supposed to be the domain of the woman, I think that she was pretty much under her husband's thumb until very recently in history. Even family life pretty much went on

under the shadow of the father as its chief figure of authority.

So I personally don't see that there's any argument with women who are making the point that the traditional division between the man who is supposed to go out and make a living and the woman who is supposed to just stay home and get pregnant and take care of herself and raise the kids and look after the house is pretty much an artificial and obsolete one these days. In this highly technological society, childbirth is no longer so arduous or life-threatening, contraception is effective and widely available and inexpensive, and most of all, the kind of work that most people do now has very little to do with a person's overall physical strength or agility. I mean, how much brute strength do you have to have to program a computer? . . .

But I do have some bones to pick with the women's movement. I do think there are some definite distortions going on in the whole thing, and some potential losses due to the women's movement in certain areas.

For one thing, and this is in some ways just a sort of academic quibble, the whole attempt to base the division of labor between man the breadwinner and woman the homemaker on anthropological analogies with man the hunter and woman the camp follower seems completely ignorant to me, maybe because I happen to know something about anthropology. My understanding is that there really is very little solid support for that differentiation that you're always hearing about, about men doing all the hunting because it was so strenuous. It just isn't that cut and dried, according to the studies I hear about, though I can't name a good one for you right at the moment.* You find women, even pregnant women, doing very heavy labor in the fields in a great many so-called "primitive" societies.

On the other hand, I don't personally believe hunting was all that macho a thing even way back in preliterate ages. I think it probably depended more on snaring and trapping, on intelligence and group cooperation, a lot more than we tend to think now. And even in cases where it didn't take a lot of people working together, I still don't think it was always so demanding that it couldn't be done by women or even children for that matter. Anyway, to me this whole idea that hunting is basically a very aggressive and highly individualistic, competitive type of activity seems like a much more recent notion. . . .

But I guess what really bothers me even more than that is that I think there are definitely some sexual role differentiations that are probably essential for human beings, and I think there's a fairly active attempt going on in some areas of the

---

*One writer who has convincingly argued that the division of food-gathering labor in many "primitive" societies was fairly equally shared by men and women is Hoffman R. Hays, author of *The Dangerous Sex: The Myth of Feminine Evil*. As Hays puts it:

> Anthropological data shows that [women] were extremely productive in certain areas. While it is true that men manufactured weapons and tools to procure and cut meat, women probably invented nets and founded the fishing industry. Women have always been associated with basketry, weaving and pottery.

The involvement of women with these crafts may well also, Hays goes on to point out, have led to the development by them of geometry, painting, sculpture, tailoring, and shoemaking. Furthermore, Hays states that women are probably the inventors of agriculture and thus the first millers and bakers. In short, the picture that Hays draws of early societies is one which, though there may be a clear-cut division of labor between men and women, it is ultimately a symbolic and equal one.

women's movement to deny them, or ignore them. Certain kinds of dominance interactions facilitate sexuality and mating. I'm not sure anyone understands just how central and crucial these types of interactions are. Some of the problems we have with women in the workplace, with efforts to get more women into more equal positions in the world of work, have to do with the conflict between built-in psychological facets of our species and the idea that work should be a sexually neutered environment, which it will never be. It is in my mind inevitable that there will develop conflicts in this area. People of the opposite sex are simply not neuter, and they never will be as long as their endocrinological systems are functioning and their glands are secreting. That isn't going to change and I suppose there will always be problems in some areas because of it. But I think they're manageable.

Another man, a Gulf Coast fisherman, had this comment:

Personally, I think the women's movement is very good. For instance, I have always thought, from the time I was quite young as a matter of fact, that parents *should* share the raising of their children, and *should* share the household chores. I remember my own father just went to work, read his paper, and that was that—he did *nothing* around the house, *nothing*. Ironically, in spite of the fact that my mother was the "protected" one, she was the one who had to do all the heavy work around the house—who had to go to the cellar to get the coal, had to beat the rugs, all that. She worked damned hard, he was just the provider. . . . I like equality. But I do *not* like a butch woman. I do not want women to become overly masculine. I want to have equality, but still

> I want a woman to be a woman. I don't want a woman to jump all over a man. Equality's fine—particularly in jobs, and in doing all the household chores together. She doesn't have to always do all the dishes, he can help her. He can wax the floors, vacuum, all that kind of thing. I personally wouldn't have any trouble adjusting to the role of being more equal. For me that would be entirely natural. I think about equality all the time—not just in terms of races, or in terms of men and women, but true equality for all of us. So if I were married, I wouldn't mind waxing the floors or something like that. That makes sense to me.

We feel there's no mistaking the authenticity of the male desire to participate equally in a general reconsideration of sex roles in this society. Over and over, men (and women) expressed to us their enthusiasm for the fact that this book would focus on representing the male point of view in the gender controversy.

Men hesitate to express this interest more publicly for a number of reasons, not only because they are severely inhibited by typically masculine fears of looking foolish, ignorant, or incompetent, but primarily because they feel deeply intimidated by the misandric undercurrents that infuse some segments of the women's movement. They resent sexist attempts to induce guilt in them purely on the basis of their gender fully as much as whites have learned to resent what are essentially racist attempts at guilt induction based on the color of their skin.

Misandry stems, we believe, from a process called repressive radicalization, which can be distinguished from its opposite, effective radicalization. Effective radicalization is fundamentally nothing more complex than classic American pragmatism. It acknowledges the functional value of mass identity and mass solidarity, but it never allows the primacy of individual self-determination to be overriden by any fixed system of ideological presuppositions.

In effective radicalization, group identity is a pragmatic issue. Rather than suppressing individual self-esteem, effective radicalization is a point of departure, a tool to be used for achieving the larger ends that facilitate individual fulfillment. Considered from this perspective, the origination of a new sense of liberated womanhood, like the formation of black pride in the 1950's and 1960's, is to the effectively radicalized individual, a clearcut means, rather than an end in and of itself.

Repressive radicalization, on the other hand, fosters a fixation on the identity of the group. It provides the most tangible reinforcement of the person's internal bulwarks against self-hatred. The result is a species of "bunker mentality," the classic condition of affiliation with others based on self-defense rather than self-enhancement. It is, in Hannah Arendt's phrase, primarily a "negative solidarity." Or as Eric Hoffer phrases it:

> The missionary zeal seems rather an expression of some deep misgiving, some pressing feeling of insufficiency at the center . . . It is a search for a final and irrefutable demonstration that our absolute truth is indeed the one and only truth.[2]

Logically following the passionate rejection of the self in Hoffer's delineation of the malevolent mass movement is its use of chauvinistic hatred as a unifying agent among its members. Projected and rationalized hatred, he points out, is particularly appropriate as a basis for the formation of greater solidarity among any group seeking relief from self-contempt:

> There is perhaps no surer way of infecting ourselves with virulent hatred toward a person than by doing him a grave injustice. That others have a just grievance against us is a more potent reason for hating them than that we have a just grievance against them. We do not make people humble and meek when we show them their guilt and cause themselves to be ashamed of themselves. We are more likely to stir their arrogance

> and rouse in them a reckless aggressiveness. Self-righteousness is a loud din raised to drown the voice of guilt within us.
> There is a guilty conscience behind every brazen word and act and behind every manifestation of self-righteousness.
> To wrong those we hate is to add fuel to our hatred . . .[3]

Plainly the repressively radicalized mentality is a self-limiting one. Its relationship to any vision of social change is based on the defensive mechanisms of denial, compensation, and displacement, rather than on a dispassionate appraisal of the self and a consequently unsentimentalized altruism.

As a secondary effect, by defining the world in absolutely negative, unredeemable terms, repressive radicalization lays the psychological groundwork for aggressive dehumanization of those who represent the status quo, by categorically indicting them as corrupt.

> The most effective way to silence our guilty conscience is to convince ourselves and others that those we have sinned against are indeed depraved creatures, deserving every punishment, even extermination. We cannot pity those we have wronged, nor can we be indifferent toward them. We must hate and persecute them or else leave the door open to self-contempt.[4]

This is the stage at which repressive radicalization acquires its most destructive potential. In the women's movement, the misandric desire to "make men pay," to create male scapegoats in order to vent frustration, is most prevalent among those susceptible to repressive perspectives. In them, this stage is typified by reverse sexism, moralistic anti-male hyperbole, ambient hostility toward all men, and a kind of gender brinksmanship in interactions with men, characterized by provocation, aggressive confrontation, and by an appetite for unilateral ultimata. Finally, the irrational tendency to interpret the historic male-centeredness of this culture as evidence of a conscious (or in Kate Millett's phrase, "ingenious") conspiracy on the part of men to persecute women and keep them in a subjugated state is at its most intense.

Reverse sexism is one of the most common features of repressive radicalization. It was without doubt the feature of the new misandry most often encountered by the men to whom we spoke and the one that left them feeling most perplexed and insulted.

Reverse sexism is any description, portrayal, or other activity that simplistically and hyperbolically depicts all men in categorical and pejorative terms: as egotistical, self-centered, foolish, arrogant, brutal, smug, insensitive, cold, childish, and so forth.

> My feelings about men are the result of my experience. I have little sympathy for them. Like a Jew just released from Dachau, I watch the handsome young Nazi soldier fall writhing to the ground with a bullet in his stomach and I look briefly and walk on. I don't even need to shrug. I simply don't care. What he was, as a person, I mean, what his shames and yearnings were, simply don't matter. It is too late for me to care.[5]
>
> —Marilyn French

Like its sexist precursor, reverse sexism functions by joining stereotyping with the desire to punish. As most of us are well aware, the combination of stereotyping and scapegoating has in many occasions in this century—though usually in societies far more overtly repressive than this one—provided both the primary justification as well as the predominant incentive for socially sanctioned brutalization, and in some instances eradication, of a hapless ethnic, religious, political, or sexual minority. As one respondent commented:

I was browsing through the new releases in a small book store. It was early in the morning, and I was the only one there, besides the clerk, a woman. I felt very relaxed and very comfortable.

Then the door opens and in walks another woman, someone I've never seen before in my life. I look up automatically, of course, a reflex action. I glance at her and, since she's a stranger, look away . . . go back to browsing.

Apparently she and the woman behind the counter are old friends. They greet each other warmly and start chatting. It's all very friendly and animated. They're not taking much trouble to speak in intimate tones, so I can't help but overhear everything they're saying to one another. Maybe I'm intruding but I don't really have much choice, and I don't really mind one way or the other. It's a fine day, after all, and I'm feeling just great.

Then the woman behind the counter begins talking about her husband, who has a cold. "It's nothing much," she says, "but he sure is sensitive about it. I don't get sick much myself, but when I do I just ignore it . . . try to keep on plugging away. Rob is just the opposite. He gets real worried and upset, like it was a personal insult to him to have a cold. God I hate to be around sick people. I just can't stand it! It makes me want to tell them to go away until they're well again."

I'm mildly surprised to hear anyone talk so uncharitably about someone you have to imagine they care for, but I remind myself that it's not my business, so I just ignore it. I stick my nose back in my book and try to go on reading again.

But then her friend laughs in a big loud booming voice, and practically shouts at me, in an unmistakably bitter tone, "Yeah, all men are just big babies. They're all *neurotics.*" There's no doubt that her comment is directed at me, so I look up again from my book—I'm the only one in the store, remember—and if looks could kill, that lady's glare would have fried me to a sizzle, right there on the spot.

Now I'm not saying women don't have some cause to be angry, but I can't see that that kind of belligerence, directed at total strangers simply because they happen to be male, is going to accomplish anything.

A trivial incident? Perhaps. But are instances of unwarranted prejudice like this one really any more insignificant than the use of "colored" instead of "black," or "girl" instead of "woman"? Few of the men we interviewed had any difficulty understanding and empathizing with the bewildered response of the browser in the anecdote above. "Sure, sure, I know the feeling," commented a black housing agency official in a large West Coast city. "It's no different than what I used to feel as a kid in Alabama walking past those crackers sitting on the porch of the local store, sitting there chewing and talking in big loud voices about little *nigras* while I scurried past."

The women we spoke with, on the other hand, tended to discount the browser's astonishment. He was invariably described by them as "whiny," "childish," or "over-reactive." We couldn't help feeling that they were perpetuating another male stereotype, that of the strong, silent male, impervious to criticism, a stereotype that puts men in a different double bind: Either they're too sensitive if they confess to being hurt by such abrasive bigotry, or they're accused of suppressing their anger if they deny being affected by it.

There are, unfortunately, other examples. For instance, in a statement reminiscent of nothing so much as sniggering male references to "tits 'n ass," the author of *Women and Madness* reduces masculinity to an equally simplistic anatomical level.

> ... men of science (and art) cannot, except momentarily and romantically, and therefore safely,

> identify strongly with their female subjects. *Their own sanity can remain firmly moored between their legs.*[6] [Italics ours.]
>
> —Phyllis Chesler

Even men's softer, more emotional sides, especially the male attitude toward romantic love (which one might reasonably expect even the most hardboiled gender radical to endorse), have been subjected to the harsh glare of repressive reassessment:

> The panic felt at any threat to love is a good clue to its political significance . . . Love is the underbelly of (male) culture just as love is the weak spot of every man, bent on proving his virility in that large male world of "travel and adventure."[7]

Though the effects of these minor flare-ups of reverse sexism are not generally grave or protracted for men, they do nothing to help recruit male support for women's rights or women's issues, and they only further aggravate the sense of estrangement from women that many men already feel. A number of the men with whom we spoke were content to dismiss such instances of blatant misandry as the work of the proverbial "lunatic fringe." Others were not so generous. They confessed to strong feelings of uneasiness and resentment: "Sometimes," said a retired Los Angeles clothing manufacturer, "it seems as if the most radical, vociferous, angry women feel that they can't achieve a satisfying sense of equality unless men pay a price for it in terms of humiliation. That bothers me. I don't want to be typecast as a jerk just because I happen to be male. So, I think, well why should I even try to get along with someone whose main interest seems to be turning me into a bad joke? I'm human too, you know."

Of course, one must acknowledge that the distinction between effective and repressive radicalization is in no way an absolute one. All processes of radicalization partake of both at different stages in their evolution, and individuals move back and forth from one to the other frequently. Many of the men we spoke with also made a point of singling out those women they knew who had, in their opinion, progressed from a repressive to a more clearly effective stance in their attitudes toward men:

> I have a female employee, a dyed-in-the-wool feminist, who was at first incredibly pugnacious and defensive about being a "liberated" woman. She had the stereotypical chip on her shoulder, like she was just waiting for you to say something remotely ambiguous about women so she could jump down your throat. The kind of person you have to walk on eggshells around. There were times early on in our working situation when she and I used to have knockdown, drag-out fights because she was so damned defensive, and she would take issue with what I had to say simply because I was a man. She would respond to my sex rather than what I had to say. Classic reverse prejudice.
> For example, I remember one time I was talking to her about a talk I had to give in Las Vegas to a group of women, all of whom were interested in going into this business. I had a brochure all worked out, and some ideas about the kinds of things I wanted to bring up, and I went in to talk to her about it. The first thing she said when I told her about the whole thing was, "What makes you think you know anything about talking to women?" You could see her face change. You could see her become instantly outraged at the idea that I could dare to be so presumptuous. All I could think of to say to her in response was "Why not, you give talks to men, what's the difference?" . . .
> But now that we've been working together for

almost two years, things have really changed. I think she saw that all I wanted to do was help her succeed, and that the reason I wanted her to succeed was because it was in my interest to do so. That made some kind of sense to her. The feminist shield and club are still there, she's ready to do battle any time, but we now have an excellent business relationship. We've had any number of really good conversations in the last year or so, and from my point of view, she's beginning to mellow. But it's been a battle. . . .

I think my wife has the black woman's approach to feminism, and that is that she's not really interested in any of this unless it works for her in a specific way. Pragmatic. Not ideological or philosophical. No banner waving. Whatever part that works for her, I'm sure that she wants to be involved in it. There's no doubt that she's been conscious of the fact that she's a female in what is pretty much a male-dominated system. That's inescapable in a field like labor arbitration where there are still only three other female mediators in the whole state.

Our feeling, shared by nearly every man we spoke to, is that at the point where a woman has thoroughly analyzed the sexist traditions of the culture she lives in, but is not especially intimidated by them, she has become effectively radicalized. She has heard the arguments of the movement's spokespeople, has encountered a broad range of feminist styles, and has assimilated those liberationist lessons that are validated by her own experience. Her sense of self-esteem, both as a woman and as a human being, is intact. She understands and respects the need that led to the creation of a renewed sense of gender dignity for women, but she does not regard it as a personal refuge, a sanctuary. She steps forward to live her life on her own terms.

What became clear to us the more we talked to people about this topic was that to the extent that masculine ratification of the women's movement has become conscious, it has also been based on a similar mixture of principles and pragmatism. In principle, most thoughtful men are predisposed to support *any* human rights movement in this country because years of civil rights activism have made it abundantly and painfully clear to the majority of American citizens that, far from being the melting pot it was represented as in grade school, this country is a complex and often dangerously unstable aggregation of many different kinds of minority factions. However, though we may now have all been successfully disabused of the myth of the process of integrating our ethnic, cultural, and sexual diversity into a viable, cohesive social whole, most of us, men and women alike, still hold some hope that greater unification of this country is possible, and they are ready to support any movement that promises to contribute to that process.

In short, there is still a fair amount of traditional American frontier egalitarianism prevalent in men, and the women's movement often tends to seem entirely compatible with its basic emphasis on individual advancement through individual self-reliance and the deliberate creation of universally equal social opportunities.

The pragmatic aspect of male endorsement of the women's movement is based on the equally American trait of frank self-interest. Though they are far less outspoken about it, men tend to share female exasperation with many aspects of conventional gender roles. Men don't necessarily like having to bear the pressures of playing breadwinner. They don't like having to work all the time. They may enjoy competition, but not as a steady diet, and not in the relentless crucible that is today's occupational marketplace. They don't like being constantly haunted by anxiety and stress. They don't like knowing that they will probably die a full decade sooner, on the average, than their female peers. They do not enjoy being strangers to their children, consistently alienated from the pleasures of guiding their development into adults. Most men would profoundly relish having more time to relax, to play, to exercise, to try things they've always wanted to do but have never been able to squeeze into packed agendas. Few men would resist changes in their roles that offered them these possibilities. But, more than anything else, most men want it to be more possible to create lasting, mutually fulfilling relationships with women.

> I think men are as bothered by this whole thing as women are. Absolutely. Just look around, at movies like *Manhattan*, or *Kramer vs. Kramer*. Those weren't just aimed at women, and they weren't as successful as they were just based on the reactions of women either. In my circle, consternation about what it is that's really going on with men and women has reached the proportions of a crisis. Well, it's funny, it's like locker room gossip, you know, where you really get down to what's on your mind. It used to be we talked about "broads" and we talked about them in what I guess would have to be described as a chauvinist way. Now we call them women, but we still talk about them, and we're more confused by them than ever. I've got friends wandering around in a state of complete befuddlement—I mean, if I've had one friend of mine I've had half a dozen tell me, "I just don't know what the hell is going on with her . . . I just don't know what to do about all this stuff."

But it is also indisputable that male involvement in the women's movement is still a wary and skeptical one. Our observation was that there was a natural and not unexpected tendency for the more conservative men among our respondents to harbor more of a suspicion that feminism would turn out to be no more durable than disco or trendy diets, that it was just one more heavily hyped American fad.

Men who feel like this, who secretly or not so secretly expect the women's movement to fade into cultural limbo, have a logical tendency to react to women's activism by wanting just to sit tight, keep their heads down, and wait it out, hoping that when the storm passes and the sociological dust settles, dispassionate appraisals of the relationship between the sexes will show that nothing very fundamental has really changed.

And there is a certain validity in this skeptical stance, at least among some men. The contact of many of them with the women's movement has until now been largely restricted to the media, which have tended to either sensationalize certain of the sexual implications of female liberation, or to focus on its more dramatic legal repercussions (e.g., lawsuits against the discriminatory practices of men's clubs and athletic teams). As a result, the movement acquires among these men a distant, abstract, somewhat surrealistic overtone. They understandably elect to wait until they find it influencing their personal, daily experiences with women before they develop a more active emotional involvement with it.

Furthermore, both men and women tend to retain a basically healthy if slightly complacent optimism about the vitality of the mutual attraction between the sexes. They find in their own experiences that reciprocated sexual interest continues, though at a more problematic level, beneath the unmistakable cloud of gender animosity that pervades our culture, and so they conclude that the gender schism is overemphasized. None of the men or women we talked to felt that the gender strife has in their experiences any of the apocalyptic overtones imputed to it by some observers, most notably George Gilder and Dorothy Dinnerstein.

Ironically, the detached, skeptical, and faintly opportunistic attitude of the average male toward the women's movement is exacerbated by the very absence of ideological aggressiveness that characterizes effective rather than repressive radicalization on the part of liberated women. For many women, feminism was the issue of the 1970's and is now in many respects behind them. For others, all the movement ever did was to articulate and legitimize their own sense of the importance of autonomy and independence in every fully human endeavor. Since such women long ago assimilated whatever they felt to be valid about feminism and then moved ahead with the business of getting on with their lives, they are understandably reluctant to label themselves staunch and active feminists. It feels vaguely regressive to them. For them, the movement has done its work. Its heyday is over. Not one of the women we spoke with in the course of these interviews wanted to identify herself as a "feminist"—all, in fact, explicitly disavowed that particular term. On the other hand, they unanimously *did* agree that they considered themselves to be more or less "liberated." As one woman explained to us:

> "I feel that the word "feminist," like the word "macho," is so emotionally loaded that it's hard to see past the activist connotations to pick up the meaning that it has to a particular woman, in a particular situation. For too many people, a "feminist" is someone in overalls driving a truck or standing on a streetcorner haranguing people. So I just don't think it's effective . . . it doesn't help me to describe myself that way.

Finally, women who are susceptible to repressive radicalization may make a point of minimizing their interactions with men, thus contributing to the slightly abstract quality that the movement has in many men's minds. In any case, the result is that men tend to have trouble distinguishing the positive effects of the women's movement on women they know, even when they happen to be married to them. As a forty-six-year-old male building contractor told us:

> I can't really say that "feminism" as I understand it, that is, a female's exhibiting behavior (including professed or demonstrated attitudes and opinions) that are not rare today but would have been unusual a generation ago, has affected my personal relationship with my wife. She works as a free-lance design consultant, and does very well at it,

but this is nothing new, sudden, or unexpected. Her model for this is one we both understand from our own mothers—her's worked full time and mine part-time when we were young. My wife has worked continuously since we were married some twenty-odd years ago, so I just don't see how her attitudes toward work could be construed as being the result of a relatively recent "feminist" awareness on her part.

His words were echoed by a senior Department of Energy official whose wife owns and operates a small acoustical design consulting business:

It's hard for me to judge the effect of the women's movement on my wife's career. It's such a chicken-and-egg kind of question. She has always been ambitious, and she's always been an excellent businesswoman. And her career was already moving ahead nicely in the late 1960's. I think the women's movement helped her, there's no doubt about that, but I also think she would have gotten to where she is today with or without the women's movement. At most what it did was to accelerate her progress. The timing was right for her because she's in a field which is dominated by men, and she has the credentials and the individual drive and personality to go far. So it all came together very neatly for her.

In other words, men may use the paradoxical invisibility of the effectively radicalized woman to justify taking a noncommittal stance toward the women's movement. They are not necessarily unsympathetic to feminist issues, nor are they for the most part dedicated chauvinists. Skeptical about the durability of sudden, massive shifts in social values, they want to wait until the movement has proven its stamina.

The primary danger in this stance, as far as we can tell, is that their lack of involvement makes these men somewhat passive, reactive, and therefore psychologically more vulnerable to role-reversal stress. By refraining from taking a more active posture in the gender debate, these men tacitly place themselves in the position of having to accommodate women's decisions to change roles and thus to adjust to the consequent changes in their own roles that ineviably follow as a result of the interdependence of men and women.

This same stance can impose passive-aggressive double-binds on women. In these cases, a clearcut double standard comes into play, one that sanctions feminist arguments when they adhere to a preconceived standard of "enlightened" egalitarian behavior, but considers them threatening when they break new ground. In other words, when activist women do something right, they're fine *human beings,* but when they do something irritating, they suddenly revert to being foolish and misguided females.

We did occasionally encounter what may have been instances of the forms of classic chauvinism exposed by the women's movement, such as the biology professor in southern Indiana who has always left housecleaning to his wife because he is "just naturally messier than women are," or the Santa Barbara stockbroker who isn't "as efficient or effective" as his wife is at cooking, cleaning, and other housekeeping chores.

Although we believe they exist, we met no men that we would describe as archetypal "male chauvinist pigs." Even the most unrepentant chauvinist seems to have learned the wisdom of public inscrutability. To the extent that the women's movement has caused some welcome inhibitions in men like these, it must already be counted a success.

Classic, blatant chauvinism probably has the fewest remaining adherents in the larger metropolitan areas of the country, especially on both coasts, and among well-educated, professional middle and upper-middle classes. This is where we did most of our interviewing. We suspect that chauvinism retains its most ardent and numerous supporters in some—but by no means all—rural areas, among lower middle-class and blue-collar families.

There are indications that even the few remaining enclaves of unapologetic masculine chauvinism may be heading for extinction. According to professor Sally Hacker of Oregon State University at Corvallis, feminist activism is intensifying in many rural areas of the country. In setting forth her explanation of this trend, Hacker points to the growth of American agribusiness and the consequent displacement of women (and men) from the traditional small farm. Forced into industrial and service-oriented employment, women who were once fully equal partners in managing a small farm suddenly find that the transition into "clerical and sales work, in factories, in poultry and meatpacking operations" imposes on them a sharper double standard in terms of wages and promotional opportunities. "So, with this increased participation, but much of it at a factory worker level, rural women are beginning to say, 'Look, this isn't fair. We're not receiving equal salaries—we don't have the same access for advancement.'"[2]

At the other end of the spectrum from outright chauvinism is the position of not only endorsing but of also actively adapting and advocating a staunchly pro-feminist point of view. In the group of men that we spoke to, those expressing this perspective tended on the whole to be younger, unmarried, without children, to have come from less traditional backgrounds, and to have less conventional occupations and aspirations.

However, we would again caution against assuming that this indicates a direct correlation between relatively greater gender liberalism and younger age. Our own initial assumption that older men would probably display a more fixed adherence to discriminatory attitudes about women and the women's movement was not borne out. To the extent that it is expressed at all, chauvinistic attitudes are as commonly held by younger as older men, and what sexism we did observe among older men tended to be extremely indirect, subdued, and perhaps even unconscious, for the most part. Signs of an unabashed sexist backlash are far more evident among teenaged males than among any of the middle-aged men we talked to.

• *The men we interviewed were most sympathetic to the economic emancipation of women, and most troubled by their sexual emancipation.*

There was absolutely no doubt in the mind of any one of the men we spoke to that a woman should receive the same pay for doing the same work as a man. To defend the opposite point of view—that women should be paid less—struck them as patently ridiculous and discriminatory.

> When you ask me whether I think women have been discriminated against, I have to say that I think it's a yes and no question. What one has to do is identify the parameters of discrimination. I think there certainly has been a tendency not to pay equal wages for equal service. Particularly in the corporate world, a woman hasn't generally been able to earn the same amount of income as her male peers. So I think materially, in the corporate area, there has been some discrimination, without question. Certainly there have been a number of cases of very successful women in the past, despite the general tendency for them to be exceptions. Mary Wells in advertising is just one example that comes to mind. But it's still news when a woman gets to the top.
>
> Generally corporate employers have tended to hold the view that the man was the breadwinner in the family and if the woman was working, it was just to supplement the family income. Now that the prevalence of the single-parent family and the presence of a lot more unmarried career women is a reality, that assumption is having to give way to contemporary lifestyles.
>
> But five years ago, the occasional unusual

woman who made it to a managerial level tended to stay right there, as a manager. And even today, there's still a strong tendency for women to get stuck at the administrative assistant level. Now that may be a very powerful position, and she may be getting very good training, say as the president's right-hand lady in a small corporation with, oh, less than a hundred people in it and less than $10–15 million in annual sales. She may be wearing four different hats and getting paid just as well as they can possibly afford to pay her, considering the revenues generated by the business, but it's still a long way from there to the very top, and, let's face it, that's still not happening to very many women.

In other fields, the same thing is true. How many female accountants do you know? Now that's a truly professional woman. How many female surgeons? How many top-level women in the sciences in general?

One of the reasons that there's been this lack is not only because of traditional assumptions about the family, but also because women have been discouraged in blatant and not so blatant ways from going to business school. It's an instructional problem. There is not a great abundance of qualified people ready to instruct this coming generation of women in many fields. That's changing of course too, in many ways. I think the opportunities are clearly greater now for young women to get some meaningful background education in business, at least as compared to ten, fifteen years ago. But in a way that begs the real question, because the real issue is the quality of instruction, and how the values of instructors may influence their teaching attitudes. Do they still think there is limited room for career women? Do they throw up their hands in horror at the thought of a woman running General Motors or being President of the United States? That's what you have to take a careful look at.

Said another man, a thirty-eight-year-old Utah optometrist, in response to our questions on economic equality for women:

In terms of discrimination, you could make a case for either point. When you talk about specifics, such as salaries, for the most part I can understand it and I agree that women have been discriminated against in that area. There was a time just a little while ago in my business—I've got six people working for me in my two branches—when I did have an employee who was male and who was doing essentially the same work as two other women I have working for me, and in the end I did offer him a higher salary than the women, but I had to really think about it pretty carefully because I wasn't sure it was justified. But he had had slightly more training than the other two had, and the real difference, at least the one that finally made it possible for me to offer him more money with a clear conscience, was that he had a wife and kid to support and these two women didn't. So I just said, well, I can't offer him the same thing these other people are making.

So I see what women are talking about when they say they're discriminated against in the job market. It's that they're running up against men who think like I do: that by and large it's still the men who are the breadwinners, and that whoever it is that's supporting a family should be making more than a single person.

Actually, it doesn't matter to me whether it's the man or the woman who's the breadwinner, but I think whoever it is, they should get more than a single person doing the same job. So the discrimination thing is complicated somewhat by that. I just don't feel I can condemn people who have paid women less over the years because it's only recently that the division of roles into man the provider and woman the homemaker has been seriously questioned and has started to change.

The men we spoke to were much less comfortable with the idea of sexual liberation for women, possibly because it was often interpreted by them as implying a blanket rejection of monogamous relationships in favor of a much more polygamous pattern of sexual behavior. There was a general, unpremeditated consensus among these men that one of the worst shocks a man could experience currently was the revelation that a woman he felt especially attracted to might want to preserve her sexual independence rather than make any kind of exclusive sexual commitment to him:

> It depends on how I feel about the individual woman. There was a time, a specific incident when I remember very clearly disliking the whole idea. That was a time when I thought this particular lady was especially fine, was really something else. I guess I kind of wanted to make her mine for awhile—call it possessiveness if you want—and she made it crystal clear that that wasn't the way she was thinking, and it really disturbed me.
> She wanted to keep playing the field—had been playing it, and intended to keep on playing it, and I guess I found out right then and there that I have an old-fashioned sense of ethics in some ways. Nothing turns me off faster than the idea that the woman I've got strong feelings for may like some other guy as much as she likes me, especially in

bed. That's an extreme turn off for me and I think it is for most other guys. I know that it's one of the things that bothers me an awful lot.

****

When I was freed from nineteen years of marriage I was terribly curious. I'm sure I had quite a bit of a double standard going for me. I wanted to move around and fool around. Just like . . . I wanted to see what it was like. I'd been brought up in a very straight background, and I had no other sexual experiences than with my ex-wife. So I wanted one-night stands, three-week stands, or whatever you want to call them, without any particular commitment going for them. Which I'm sure was very common. But—although I might not have been able to say this, I'm sure I felt it—I felt negative about the idea that a woman might take this same attitude. It didn't seem right to me. It still doesn't in some ways. I didn't think they should feel that way and I still question it. Emotionally, it's very difficult for me to accept.

But they happen to be doing it anyway. I remember one woman saying to me, "I just want you to know that you're not exclusive with me. I have a number of boyfriends and if they happen to come to town, I would feel free to go to bed with them."

It was like a knife cutting straight into my heart. I couldn't say anything. I felt nauseous. I choked. *Intellectually*, I could understand it. *Emotionally*, I couldn't stand it. It's been three years now since that particular incident, and I'm still not able to cope with that kind of thing, and I'm not sure I ever will be. I don't know if this particular issue will ever get resolved on an "equal" basis at all, at least for the men I know. We may get more tolerant, but I really don't think a woman, no matter how much freedom they have, will ever be truly free in that particular way. Maybe if anybody should change, it should be men who become less promiscuous, not women who become more so. If women have all the economic and political freedom in the world, I don't think their sexuality is ever going to be free in that sense.

Although it is still in general an uncomfortable topic for most men, some of those we talked to are beginning to become much more aware of their feelings of jealousy, and much more willing to verbalize them.

> . . . Then a couple of months ago, I finally broke down and called her. I was lonely, sure, but I was also man enough—no, better make that *human* enough—to know that I wanted to do something about the situation, not just ignore it, or pretend that it didn't exist. That seemed too chickenshit to me. So I called and asked her out to dinner and we had delicious steaks, wine, and toward the end of the dinner, she looked at me indifferently and kind of coldly said, "You can come back to my place if you'd like"—I know her hard-boiled act. Sometimes it's just a coverup for feeling anxious, but not always. This time, looking back on it with hindsight, I think it was just plain indifference. But I kept at it, working hard to get her to soften up, to warm up to me, staying cheerful, staying as charming as I can, and we were beginning to talk it out, to get through it, to get down to the anger and resentment. So we got back to her place and we both knew, without having to say anything to one another, that we were going to head for bed as soon as we got through the front door. I mean we'd

been together almost constantly for four years before the separation and we didn't have to spell everything out. We just knew.

God, I remember the next parts all so vividly. I went into the bathroom, came out, went into the bedroom, started unbuttoning my shirt, slipping out of my shoes, and nearly ran into Barb as she stepped out of the door to the kitchen. I took one look at her face—she was crying—and I knew things were really wrong, really bad, really over. She was completely beside herself.

"I've got something to tell you," she said, or something like that. She was staring into my eyes, and holding my arms at my sides. I went numb, I think I already knew then what she was going to say, and I began to feel that feeling of absolute horror creeping through me. So then she said—I should add that it was obvious that she was really in a lot of pain herself—she said, "I went out, while we were apart, with the guy across the hall. He's just split up with his wife, he misses his kids, we got to talking one day, had a few drinks, came back here and . . . I slept with him. I felt sorry for him."

That was easily the worst emotional shock of my life. I could see it coming and it still hurt like hell. Somehow I'd never imagined *me* feeling jealous before. It just seemed like such a cliche. And even when we were living apart, I kind of subconsciously assumed that Barb wouldn't be fooling around because of the kids. So it was really a devastating shock to hear this from her. Just hearing her say the words, "I slept with him" was more appalling than I can describe. And they had an immediate, devastating physical effect on me.

Like I say, I'd never even imagined being jealous before. And even if this was the early 1970's, I thought I was pretty enlightened, not much of a chauvinist, pretty liberated. Intellectually, I wouldn't have dreamed of defending sexual monogamy. It just didn't seem to mean much anymore, so I kind of unconsciously dismissed it. After that experience with Barb, though, let me tell you, it means something very, very powerful to me, something I completely believe in, though I'm still not sure I could find a solid rational defense for it. Paternity, wanting to be certain of the paternity of a kid, that's about the best argument for it I can imagine, but even that one doesn't cut it anymore. I don't know. There's something else at work there that is stronger than any rational argument I can concoct. I just don't think most of us are ready for polygamy, or whatever you'd call it. Certainly not most of the men I know.

There was not only the shock of feeling jealous, but also the shock of noticing that I was feeling jealous, something I just never expected to feel. So you could say as well as being a devastating experience, it was also a revelation.

Physically it hit me in the stomach. You know the phrase, "it wrenched my guts"? That's what it did. Literally. That's what it felt like, like I was being torn apart in the middle. It made me feel dizzy and nauseous at the same time, like I was going to throw up and black out, all at the same time. I do remember actually stumbling back past Barb to the bathroom and slamming the door and then hanging over the toilet, waiting to vomit. Eventually I think I came out and just left, kind of like sleepwalking, I don't even know if I said anything to her or not. But I didn't see her again for years.

Sensing that their very powerful drive for sexual exclusivity cannot be defended on reasonable grounds, that there is little rational merit in their resistance to the idea that women should have as much right as men to sexual self-determination, many men overreact by denying their monogamous impulses and struggling to conform to what they imagine is an enlightened lack of concern about the sexual prerogatives of their female partners. Unfortunately, in all too many cases this suppression of their true sexual anxieties collapses with devastating psychological effects when the woman behaves consistently and openly engages in multiple sexual relationships.

> This whole issue of sexual agreements is a strange one for me because I've been full circle with it. I came from a very conservative rural New England family, where there was just no question of the possibility of having affairs in a marriage because adultery was a sin and the people I grew up around took their religion very seriously. So when I came out to the Midwest to go to drama school, I wasn't really expecting the kind of dramatic shift in sexual thinking that came along in the late 1960's. I thought I was pretty knowledgeable, sophisticated, you could say, in a sense, but . . . well, when I first heard about feminism in the late 1960's, I thought it was a crock. I don't exactly know why it struck me that way, but it sure did. Mainly I guess it was because it seemed like they were making such a big deal out of something I wanted to think of as more or less natural. I'm sure there was also some kind of psychological threat involved in it, but I remember feeling extremely bored with what I thought at the time was a very obvious and clumsy attempt on the part of feminists to interpret making love as a political act.
> But as more time went by, it began to affect me in a completely different way. I took some feminist seminars, never quite really knowing what I was

doing there, read everything I could get my hands on that had to do with women and women's rights and that kind of thing, and talked to women about it. Eventually some things about it began to make more and more sense, in a very subtle, undramatic sort of way. It never became any kind of cause for me, per se, but I could really begin to see how this culture's view of male-female relationships could be construed as being way too narrow, especially in terms of the double standard. I just couldn't see why women had to be more confined sexually than men, especially with contraception being so much more effective and available.

But anyway, I had gotten into a pretty close relationship with a woman named Monica while I was at school, and she came with me when I graduated and came to New York. She was about four years younger than me, but very precocious in certain ways. Maybe I should say intellectually precocious, because in other ways she had a very hard time dealing with the real world. She thought it was a real pain in the ass, which it is for me too. She'd take a job, keep it for six months, then just quit one day and never talk about it again. I guess she just felt inferior, intimidated by the world. Anyway, she didn't really have a lot of strong social attachments to society in general.

As a result, in the relationship with her, I tended to become her screen, her medium for dealing with life out there. That was the first time I'd ever been really fully into that role, and I found I actually kind of like it, at least on some levels. It was like playing the classic provider. I guess . . . my image is that she's in the bedroom and I'm out here dealing on the street, out on the level with the money, and the deals, and the work. She's several removes from dealing with anything out here, and I'm out in the middle of it. Kind of weird.

Well, eventually we got married, but partly because of that exposure to feminism I'd had I started to want her to become more independent. Maybe we were just *too* close in some ways. It began to seem more and more claustrophobic to me. In a lot of ways, consciously and unconsciously, I started to try to create more space, more breathing space for both of us. Pushing her away, pushing her out. And it went so far as to push her to have other sexual relationships, partly, I admit, because I wanted to have a little more of that kind of freedom myself. It was also starting to feel like she was so close to me, she was so much a part of me that I really couldn't see her clearly or feel anything for her anymore. But if someone else came on to her, whether it was territoriality or just perversity or what I don't know, it re-ignited my interest in her. Some kind of vicarious way of appreciating her began to emerge in me.

So I know I did a lot of things to set up the groundwork for her to become interested in other men. It's a little fuzzy in my mind now, since we went through so much about it later, so many stages of accusation and reconciliation, but one thing I remember is that I kept kind of teasing her about how she'd only made love to one other guy before she married me, and that I'd had lots of lovers, even a few while we were first going out together, which she had found out about and which had made her feel very hurt and outraged. So I kind of egged her on, made her feel like she might be missing something.

But anyway, I was completely absorbed in working and rehearsing, and she didn't have a job so she just stayed home a lot and went to a dance class, or cooked these incredible gourmet meals for $2.95 worth of ingredients, that kind of thing. She had a pretty good life and she could do lots of creative things, though we weren't rich. But she wasn't happy, she wanted more attention and I just didn't have time to give it to her. So I think on her part she felt betrayed and rejected by all the time I was putting into my career.

I was totally into it, and knew I had to be completely devoted to it, so finally I started encouraging her to go out with this friend of mine, an older man, in his late forties then, almost twice her age. He was quite wealthy and lonely. So they'd go to the movies or out for a drink, do all those things I didn't have time for. I felt good about it at first, because I didn't have any real demands on her time and she was cooking meals and keeping up her end of the housekeeping chores pretty well. And she didn't see him all that often. It wasn't like a big romance or anything like that. And she did like him a lot, liked being with him. And he liked her. I thought it was harmless.

And then after a couple of months, I kind of noticed that she was never around the house in the evenings. It seemed like they were *always* together, always going out to dinner or something, and I started to feel left out, a little lonely.

Then we were together one evening, alone, just the two of us, and there was some kind of definite tension in the air, and she told me she was sleeping with him. Things just spilled out. She just came out with it. I was totally shocked. I remember feeling like, oh my God, like the whole bottom of my stomach dropped out, like, wait a minute, you weren't supposed to take it *that* seriously. And that was a revelation for me, because, like I say, even though I had kind of pushed her into it, had kind of urged her to do it, had set it up, with the assumption that, you know, what was good for the gander was good for the goose—if I wanted more sexual freedom, it only seemed fair that she should have it too—but when it came down to facing the fact that she was sleeping with someone else, that wasn't how I felt at all. I was outraged and shocked, and horrified. I went through a lot of real pain, psychological and physical. The final outcome was that I insisted she cut it off. Once I found out it was sexual, I couldn't handle it. I insisted she stop. And then it got very hard for him, for my friend Steve, because he had gotten very attached to her, and wanted to marry her, and yet he felt very guilty about the way he was deceiving me. But I didn't even want her to see him to say good-bye. I insisted that she just write him a letter. He finally came over and we talked it out, but it was agonizing. Finally it cooled down, and it actually made our relationship work much better, but now I don't really believe that open-marriage type arrangements can work for most people. There's just too much pain involved.

Masculine confusion over female sexual emancipation is even further complicated by a widespread male ambivalence over the assumption by women of the initiating role in sexual contacts. For many men, the new aggression and candor on the part of women in meeting their sexual appetites is clearly threatening. It makes them feel extremely uncomfortable and pressured. As one of our interview participants, a forthright Montana ranchhand, commented:

Women are now demanding a whole lot more from the sexual encounter than they used to, because they've been exposed to the fact that there's a whole lot more to it than they learned from Mom, at least as I remember what Moms were like when I was a youngster. It's not the same to them, or at least they've been led to think it's not the same, or shouldn't be the same, whether it really is or not, and a guy knows that they feel different expectations from sex, because that's just about all you read or hear about these days.

So you suddenly feel, I'm really being put on the spot now. I've got to live up to what this woman thinks is supposed to happen, that she's been led to expect.

When I think back to when I was a youngster, the whole thing was just to get to the point of actually doing it. Once you got there, nobody gave much of a thought to their partner, except you just knew you were going to drive each other mad, and it didn't really matter whether you actually did or not because you for sure knew you were having the time of your life. Nobody thought that much about checking on how it was going while you were in the middle of it because you just assumed you were driving each other mad. Sure, sometimes the woman might fake it, but not all that often. They weren't all that intimidated by men, no more than they are now.

Seems a little cold-blooded to me, the way it goes now. Sure there was some hypocrisy back then, some women just acted like they were all caught up in it, just so they could get married and settle down and have a house and raise a family, but now it seems like it's gotten all clinical. Now it's the other way around: Women not only aren't going to fake it, they're trying to supervise all the time. "Now do this, no, not like that, like this . . . now do that." A little of that kind of thing goes a long way. It spoils the romance, if you know what I mean. Turns sex into another chore.

And another thing, women are gossiping about men. They're more likely now to talk to their friends about things that used to be private, to say something like, "He was a good lay, he was a lousy lay." I've had it happen to me. You're sitting there at a table at some party and everyone's talking and you're minding your own business and you hear some woman say to her friend, braying across the table, "Yeah, but he's a lousy lover." They really do. And they exchange notes on men, on how they do in bed. It's kind of funny, but it's kind of sad too. It doesn't seem like progress to me, it seems like just the same thing we were doing as kids thirty years ago, except now it's the other way around. It's the women who are doing what the men used to do.

Anyway, that's the kind of thing that puts a lot of pressure on you in the actual sexual encounter. More so people my age I imagine than the ones who are in the generation that grew up after the pill, I guess. Anyway, back in my day we spent all our time trying to get 'em there, and didn't generally have any time to sit down and do instant replays on the spot because when it finally did happen we were so worked up we couldn't hardly see straight. It only took a few minutes and we didn't know where we were. Of course, it always went too fast, and that's something I'm glad has changed. Now that we have the pill, and other kinds of better birth control, and young women aren't so worried about getting pregnant anymore, they've started thinking, "Why can't I play around too?" That's an attitude that has its pluses for men, because it means they're more able to take their time, things aren't so hard to get to the point where they're in bed. Instead of just on and off, with the whole thing being so competitive, being such a struggle, they can try to be better lovers, can relax a little more.

But the thing of it is, at least for guys over thirty-five or so, they're not really adjusted to it yet. I can't speak for younger guys, like I say, but for men in my generation, you get a lot more situations where anxiety comes into play for the male in sex these days. Women may have anxiety in sex too, but it's not going to put them on the spot so much. Unless there is something pretty wrong with them organically, they are still able to perform, to fulfill their end of the deal if that's what's going on. And if they really want to, they can still act in order to make the guy feel he was great and so on.

A man can't. He can't fake making love. Oh, he can work at it and be very good at it, and can probably fulfill most of what a woman wants without ever getting an erection, but in most guys' minds, you're not really making love unless you get it up. So now, someone like me, who didn't have to think too much about sex in these sorts of ways when I was a youngster, he's liable to have more anxiety about it now.

Confirming the current view of most sex researchers that impotence has become a very prevalent symptomatic response to this sense of pressure from sexually liberated women, all but one of the women that we spoke to agreed that intermittent stress-related impotence had become a much more common occurrence in their own sexual experiences in recent years. This comment was typical:

> I got to be great friends about a year ago with an editor, a man in his late forties, we got to be friends, we really liked each other, and we went to bed together. He couldn't get an erection, though

there's nothing wrong with him. He said it was because he was intimidated by me. I didn't think I was acting at all aggressive, but he told me stories about other women, about growing up in New Jersey, being in a gang, and how much he liked women and was always after women. And then he'd been married for years and years, then he got a divorce and everything had changed, women had changed, and how instead of waiting for him to say, "yes, yes, yes," they were jumping in first and saying, "yes, yes, yes" to him and it scared him.

However, masculine jealousy and complaints about extreme female sexual assertiveness were by no means the only responses we got to our questions about women's new sexual independence. There was also a definite contingent of men in our sample who wanted women to take on even more of the responsibility for initiating sexual contacts, and who felt that most women had thus far been shirking this aspect of true sexual equality. These men made it very clear that they strongly resented always having to play the approach role in sexual encounters. Said one of them, a thirty-three-year-old sailmaker:

> I'm a big supporter of women's liberation. I really believe in it. But I feel they are way behind in one area. I know only a couple (literally *two*) women who have ever made it a point to take the initiative in going out and picking up guys, of making the first move. Women may try it once or twice, but they give it up fast. This pisses me off because they're not doing their share. I mean it. They're not risking rejection. They're playing it safe. They're not doing their share to bring us together. It's not fair for the man to *always* have to make the first move.

Another man, a fifty-six-year-old computer programmer, echoed these sentiments and added:

Nine times out of ten the first overt sexual move is made by the male. I mean, sure, some women, particularly those who aren't involved with a man—they may have said to themselves, once or twice, "All right, I'm going to do like a man, I'm gonna go out and get laid." But ninety percent of the time if you go out on a date, the first overt move, ignoring who wants what and the differences between seduction and aggression—is always made by the man.

It gets boring to be the aggressor all the time, the initiator. That's why relationships go sour. And it's not just in terms of sex. It applies to everything. If you only play one role all the time, it's bound to come to an end. There are rooms in your personality you haven't looked at yet, and the more you stay stuck in one role, the more frantic you get to feel about being shut off from them.

I think it's fine that men do the initiating maybe fifty-one percent of the time, but then it would be nice to have times when a woman takes over and says, "Let's do this!" I've found very few women, even among the so-called liberated ones, who are really willing to make a decision like, I want to go to this movie tonight, and let's go! Even women who've made a lot out of feminism, when it comes right down to it, they feel like, "Why isn't this guy calling me up all the time? Doesn't he like me? Why should I have to call him?" They feel degraded, somehow, by having to put themselves out, having to risk rejection in ways that they feel they shouldn't. They're spoiled.

And in fact men *do* still make almost all the first moves in dating and courtship, according to the available studies. Women may sometimes expedite, or "engineer," those moves by making themselves available, responding with special vivaciousness to a particular man's casual attentions, contriving apparently impersonal reasons to call or otherwise interact with him, and so on, but even in "singles" bars, where people are present ostensibly to meet members of the opposite sex, women almost *universally* wait for men to initiate contact.

It is worth noting that some men we interviewed were enthusiastically in favor of the classic feminine strategy of seduction as the most effective way for women to communicate sexual availability. Explained a Georgetown attorney we spoke with:

> Women take the initiative in the process of making sexual contact by signaling their receptivity, and they can do so very effectively. I had a woman walk into my office unannounced one day not so long ago and then immediately start to back out, saying something like, "Oh excuse me, you must be busy." For some reason, I said, "Oh, no, please stay," because in that fraction of a second of eye contact, I had sensed something about her. Eventually we made love that night, and she later admitted that she had been intending to lure me on, to give me a green light, as it were. But I was the one who had made all the forward, explicit moves. As far as I'm concerned, there's nothing criminal about that division of sexual roles. It's not demeaning to women to use that kind of subtlety, as far as I can see. Nor is it manipulative. Furthermore, I think it's a definite turn off for women to play a heavy handed aggressive role in sexual approach situations. Why it should even be advocated at all when the female power to sexually attract is so damn persuasive is a complete mystery to me.

Nonetheless, for the men in our sample who resented having to initiate contact with women, the facts bear out that they are most often required to do so. Only one man among those we talked to had ever been asked for a date by a woman (an ingenious telephone company employee who installed his new telephone and thus had his phone number already at hand). The Gallup organization reported in December 1979 that among working women over twenty-five with annual incomes of over $20,000, only one in four had ever asked a man out for a meal and picked up the check.

Understandably, no one likes to risk sexual rejection, but these men feel they are still having to bear more than their fair share of this anxiety. Doing so tends to make them cynical about the women's movement, about women who are opportunistic about sexual liberation: autonomous and assertive when it suits them, when they have little to lose, but coy and passive when assertion would mean running the risk of losing rather than gaining, of getting turned down rather than turned on.

- *None of the men we interviewed anticipate the emergence of a male counterpart to the women's movement—i.e., a "men's liberation movement."*

As far as we can tell, the efforts to date to develop such a movement have enjoyed very limited success. We suspect that most of the men who have participated in them have done so from a sense of curiosity rather than commitment. If the very definite lack of enthusiasm among the men we spoke with is a reliable indication, changes in men's roles will not come about as the result of the appearance of a relatively unified mass movement. In our opinion, most men are still far too individualistic to make such a movement feasible:

> To be perfectly honest, I do feel superior to the type of person who needs a cause, or some gigantic organization to belong to, a group. I just don't feel it . . . you know, I did belong to a gigantic group once, and I got out of it as soon as I possibly could: The United States Army.

> I've had a very difficult time in my life over

feeling that I really belonged to anything. I had a tough time at college. I remember I joined a fraternity, thinking that I was pretty gregarious and got along with people real well, but as soon as I did I thought it was a big mistake that I had joined. I didn't know that much about myself back then.

Even today, I don't feel the brotherhood of being a broadcaster with others. I don't want to feel any "brother" anything. I feel I'm not meant to be a member of anything. I'm a long distance runner and I run marathons. As soon as a marathon is over, I don't feel any feeling like I want to hang around and say, "Hey, we're all marathoners here together." I just want to get the hell out of there. . . .

I would react rather negatively, if someone said, "Here's a men's liberation movement, why don't you join?" because I think that things are done personally. I think they are really done individually. I don't believe in movements like that. If you need the help of a movement, then you're saying it won't work unless you all get together. And I don't think that's true. I don't believe it, for me or for most men.

I think it may be true in certain areas, such as if women didn't make a storm about getting equal pay, they wouldn't be getting it. But becoming equal in your head, or to become free in your head, in your attitude toward yourself, is an individual thing.

And it doesn't come about as a result of joining a club or becoming part of a movement. I really am very skeptical of anything that has all kinds of special jargon and a clubby, in-group effect. Let's say est, all this stuff, I'm very doubtful of it. It's temporary and it's gimmicky.

I think the fundamental truths of living are very simple. I mean life is complex, but I think if you can't reduce issues to a very simple level, then that's wrong. Also, I know for a fact that there's a world of opportunists out there taking advantage of the plight of unhappy men and women right now, and all they're really doing is offering new labels, putting people into all these little groupie boxes—you can name dozens of different groups that are essentially offering new names for the same old thing. . . .

Certainly more men need new options, fresh ways to go about enriching their lives, as much as women do. There's no doubt that most men want fuller, more effective, yet at the same time more lasting relationships with women. We know from these conversations that they are willing to adjust and adapt a great deal to achieve these aspirations. It is probably true that men have traditionally underestimated the central role that emotional self-reliance plays in creating new options for oneself. Without really knowing it, men have often relegated the nurturing functions in relationships to their female partners and have as a result become blindly, childishly dependent on them for emotional sustenance. As Herb Goldberg has acutely observed, it seems clear that "well-founded and self-caring, meaningful change and growth for men can only happen if they develop same-sex support systems that would lighten their dependency on women and would also allow them to go through whatever changes they need to go through without fear of alienating their sole source of intimacy."[9]

Marc Feigen Fasteau has also commented on the male tendency to become emotionally dependent in his primary relationships with women. He notes that the disparity between the masculine image of controlled, rational self-confidence and men's inability to deal with their own or their wives' unhappy feelings evokes more contempt in women than anything else.

> Of all the areas in which men fail women, this is the one that cuts the deepest and, ultimately, evokes the most contempt. Nothing contrasts more

sharply with the masculine image of self-confidence, rationality, and control than men's sulky, obtuse, and, often virtually total, dependence on their wives to articulate and deal with their own unhappy feelings, and their own insensitivity, fear, and passivity in helping their wives deal with theirs. This, more than anything else, disillusions women about their men. Bromides like "Men are just overgrown little boys" are both a description of the phenomenon and an attempt, by labeling it innocuously, to ease the pain of disillusionment: disillusionment at having subordinated yourself to a person who isn't, it turns out, special enough to justify the sacrifice, who is probably not much smarter than you are in most ways and in some very important ways is a lot less perceptive, more dependent, and more childlike.[10]

Our conversations with men in no way contradicted the basic views of Goldberg, Fasteau, and others, the position that there is a clear need for men to now concentrate on developing what might be called a stronger sense of emotional self-sufficiency, i.e., less dependence on women for support in the face of pain and disappointment. Older men in particular tended to display a strange blind spot when it came to expressing a sensitive grasp of their own psychologies. They appeared either to deny completely or exhibit at most a very limited appreciation of their nurturance needs. Having been conditioned to deprecate the value of understanding their own emotional topographies, men will benefit from the relaxation of rigid role models and expectations instigated by the women's movement. To reiterate our central point here, we strongly doubt that this will occur within the context of a mass movement.

Furthermore, as Herb Goldberg has commented, the construction of new role models for men must avoid the tendency to unthinkingly ape patterns of the women's movement."[11]

Among other concerns, Goldberg's fear is that new expectations for a "liberated" male will only add to the already severe role pressures most men face by creating a new type of corrosive competitiveness—Who can become the most liberated man of all? Such competitiveness would only serve to perpetuate rather than mitigate male role stress. Pursuing this new role model singlemindedly, as though it were yet another achievement cue, he would only intensify this sense of gender estrangement.

In fact, there is already a trend in many areas toward the development of excessively literal-minded masculine over-compliance with "the expectations of liberated women." In many cases it is causing women, *especially* those who have been effectively radicalized by the movement, a surprising and paradoxical sense of frustration.

One of the women we spoke to who articulates this experience well is Laura Gerrard, an attractive and successful Chicago attorney in her mid-thirties. Laura firmly describes herself as a liberated woman, and can recite a long catalogue of feminist "firsts" that she helped inaugurate in Illinois. She also, however, is quick to add the disclaimer that she is not a militant, "kneejerk" activist—and that she finds herself reappraising some of the codes of behavior that she once felt were automatically implied by her role as an emancipated woman.

> More and more often these days I find myself deeply missing a certain kind of masculine assurance, a kind of strong, confident style—*ego* even, if that's what it amounts to. The men I'm around seem too deferential to me, too hesitant, too damned *timid* these days! They think it's consideration or something, but half the time it just makes me feel awkward and angry. . . .
>
> Either that or it's this kind of man that I've started to call California Passive—you know, kind of easy to get along with, acts slightly stoned, whether or not he's actually doing any drugs, "mellow," and basically passive.

I want to be around men who aren't afraid to let their sexuality show, who are willing to come on to me, to let me know that they desire me and would be happy to pursue me. I don't think that necessarily makes me into a sex object . . . I know, I know, I realize I'm contradicting the great dictum, Thou Shalt Not Treat Woman As Sex Object, but I think we all realize now that that's just not possible, or even desirable. Men and women are sexual beings, and they always will be. For that matter, I see plenty of women treating men as sex objects—you know that a forty-five-year-old woman with a twenty-two-year-old boyfriend is interested in him for the same reason that a forty-five-year-old man dates a woman half his age: sex.

Sex *object?* No, of course not, especially not with strangers. But sexual *being?* Most definitely.

Somehow I think many woman have managed to give men the impression that to be sexually alive to a woman is to insult her. Granted, the traditional smug, uninvited, sniggering form of male sexual come-on is boorish and crude. But gracious erotic attention, frank interest, subtle flattery, compliments, all that, are a long way from crude innuendo in my book. I guess that's what men have to learn: the simple human difference between considerate, active sexual interest and derogatory, sexist condescension.

It would be crazy for me to deny that I want those little grace notes that used to highlight my contacts with men . . . small things, gentlemanly things, gestures like holding doors open for me, bringing me thoughtful little gifts, insisting on paying for dinner now and then. Frankly, I'm sick of this compulsive insistence on, uh, *symmetry* between the sexes. It's turned all of my recent relationships into perfectly dreadful minuets. If I cook a dinner, he has to cook one; if he disrobes me in the evening, then the next night it's my turn to undress him for bed.

I had one friend, an ex-lover from the past, ask me out to dinner a couple of weeks ago. He came by, it was nice to see him, we went out to dinner, it was pleasant. I enjoyed his company. But then at the end of the meal, the check came, and he got very stiff and said, "Look, Laura, if we're going to spend the night together, I want you to pick up half the check." He really did. I was flabbergasted. It wasn't that it was wrong for him to feel that way, but it was such a damned insensitive thing to say at that moment, it made me want to laugh, or cry, or something. I was so frustrated. It made me feel like he was saying, You're going to have to pay if you want to play. I mean, it gets pretty mechanical.

It strikes me as I talk to you that it's basically an accountant's mentality: debit, credit, tit-for-tat, balanced emotional books at the end, everything neatly worked out, tidy and reciprocal. It's boring. It makes me feel that I can't ever just let myself go and surrender to being coddled and pampered, which I love and feel I deserve now and then. When I do give in to it, I feel vaguely guilty, as though my credentials as a card-carrying liberated woman were suspect . . . a "traitor to the cause" kind of feeling. Like I say, that's crazy!

More and more women like Laura seem to be feeling that their desires for autonomy and their ways of asserting it are coming into distinct conflict with their equally strong desires to establish a solid, lasting, committed relationship with a man they can love and respect.

"Love and respect" can be difficult to develop in a climate of rapidly changing role values. The growth of what appears at times to be a slightly regressive nostalgia among women for "real men" has been widely remarked on recently. As Dr. Wolfgang Lederer, author of *Fear of Women*, comments: "Yes, even the women want men to be manly; in fact, what enrages the feminists even more than male chauvinist behavior, is the abdication of men, their metamorphosis from brutes to whimps [sic].[12] In *The New Male*, Herb Goldberg quotes a letter that appeared in the *Village Voice* from a twenty-seven-year-old man who was by nature gentle and non-aggressive, but who found that his chances of picking up women in singles bars were greatly enhanced if he dressed and acted the part of a stereotypical macho male.[13]

Some women try to suppress their doubts about the possibility of finding a relationship with a man that is satisfying within the context of the women's movement. But they find that the relationships they want elude them. Others seem simply to give up, to become cynical, telling themselves that such a relationship is another patriarchal hoax. Most, however, feel a persistent sense of unhappiness at the estrangement between the sexes. Said another woman we talked with:

> The real sensitive men I meet try so hard to be understanding that they don't assert themselves at all. They're so lacking in confidence about their role and their identities as men that the whole issue becomes very confusing. I think it just makes women in the movement who tend to be aggressive anyway get even more aggressive for men to be so diffident. One feeds the other in a kind of negative symbiosis.
>
> It's been painful for me for some time that it's been mostly women that I've been very close to. The kind of hopes and fears I've had, the kind of real vulnerable issues that anyone experiences now and then, it's been only other women that I've been able to share them with, not men. That's sad.

Added another woman:

You know, it's odd, but I understand that feeling of nostalgia for the good old days before the women's movement—at least I think I do—and even share it to some degree myself. I think it comes up because we imagine that before the advent of a real sense of sexual liberation, men's and women's roles were clearly defined in a way that, while it was somewhat limiting, wasn't in many ways as limiting as what often seems to be the sheer sexual chaos we see around us now.

Partly it's the obvious fact that rules at least give us a clearcut sense of when we're conforming and when we're not, and by doing so they give us a sense of reassurance. We know where we stand. The convention may be that men and women do not sleep together until they are married and after they're married they don't sleep with anybody else. Now that may or may not be what men and women actually do, what their real, true-life behavior actually is, but having that convention as a common value at least lets everyone know, without any question, when they're conforming to social mores and when they're not. And there's something to be said for that, hypocritical as it may sound in some ways.

The other thing, though, a much more important thing in my view, is that we've lost the knack of how men and women can be friends. It was actually easier when they knew they could safely assume they weren't going to sleep together. After liberation, no one is really sure what any of our traditional social cues mean. If you go out with someone, does it mean that you're inviting sex with them, or that you've consented in advance to their proposing sex, or what? There are no clear guidelines, it's up to the individuals involved to make them up for themselves as they go, and that freaks a lot of people out.

It's not so hard on single people, who go out all the time, and are well-practiced, who have well-developed repertoires of how to make suggestions in a subtle but clearcut way, but for other people, like men who have just split up with their wives, *particularly* those who have been dumped by their wives and are feeling a little ego-shattered already, it's extremely difficult to go out and take the risks that go along with learning these new social skills, those that go along with effective dating, or whatever it's being called now.

It's a cyclic thing, of course. Social rules get too tight for people to conform to them, for some reason, so they don't, and then the rules are seen as hypocritical, and there's a revolt and they're tossed out. But they always creep back in. Have you noticed that formal etiquette is making a comeback? It's because people are tired of social anarchy. They want rules. If there are no rules, there's so much confusion, so much ambiguity, and so much energy has to go into straightening it out and trying to figure situations out that people get tired and fed up and then you get a backlash. Which in turn can go too far and start to head for too much rigidity again, but for the time being I think that's the least of our worries.

Women, seeking to advance from a position of disadvantage, need the powers of mobilization and momentum that accompany the formation of group solidarity in order to break free of the role-bound inertia that they will no longer tolerate. Men need something else, a loosening and relaxing of the furious occupational momentum that most of them have been forced to cultivate in order to meet their responsibilities as breadwinners. They need a chance to relax and unwind, to detoxify from the economic crucible that has forged their lives until now. The true promise of the women's movement in their eyes is that it may enable women to become fullfledged partners in this sphere of life as well.

In researching this book, we often heard it said that the women's movement was "all about options." As men like Herb Goldberg have repeatedly pointed out, men need more options too. Although many traditionally "masculine" values seem like honest and valuable options for both sexes, the aggressive mentality that insists on defining the world as a competitive scramble for the elusive top of the heap and the pyrrhic appellation of "winner," a mentality that has historically relegated whole classes of people—blacks, Hispanics, the elderly, and of course, women—to the sidelines, strikes us as fundamentally impoverished. Our material resources may be limited, but our intelligence, imagination, and inventiveness certainly are not. We all need liberation from this state of mind. In the long run, the truest contribution of the women's movement may be to help us do that.

Our conversations with these men lead us to not only concur with Goldberg's conclusions but to add to them our feeling that the changes that men may undergo in the next few years will not be in any way systematic or universal. These changes will be private and will occur within the unique circumstances of each man's life. The most basic work that will be done in liberating themselves will be done in the one-to-one setting provided by the couple, where men feel most secure about risking the exposure of their doubts and fears.

• *Though they were unable to define concisely what they meant by these terms, every one of the men we talked to unequivocally affirmed the existence of a fundamental, significant, and inescapable distinction between "masculinity" and "femininity." It was clear from their attempts to explain what they meant by this distinction that they believe that biological gender distinctions have important and incontrovertible psychosociological ramifications.*

The experiences of most men have convinced them that there is a fundamental psychophysiological basis for gender, and that it implies—if not dictates—consequential differences between masculine and feminine attitudes, behavior, cognition, emotion, and sexuality. However, an intriguing difference appeared between the way men and women interview subjects responded to our intentionally vague question: "Do you think there is anything inherent in human sexual differentiation that corresponds to the connotations of the terms 'masculinity' and 'femininity,' or are these simply references to obsolete role models?" Without hesitation, men unanimously and immediately said, yes, they definitely believed that there was a difference between men and women that transcended the level of basic anatomy and which had important implications for the formation of individual psychology and the configuration of larger social contexts. Women universally responded to this question with the obvious counter-question requesting further clarification, e.g., "What do you mean by 'masculinity' and 'femininity'?"

In spite of semantic questions most of the women we spoke to about differences between men and women felt the same way as the men. Said one:

> Looking at it in a very earthy way, when you think of what happens to a man and a woman sexually, the woman gets softer and the man gets harder. And that seems to be the way it's supposed to be, at some level. That sure doesn't mean that women all have to be sweet and soft, barefoot and pregnant, while all men have to be rough and tough, macho strong and silent. But when we struggle against the male-female differences as much as we have been, we just overcompensate. We get women pouring cement and crushing beer cans while men get more and more narcissistic and spend all their time worrying about their sagging jaw lines. One's as bad as the other. Total role

reversal is as silly as the traditional stereotypes . . . There's just a lot of unhappiness now.

In other words, men believe that there is something inescapably female about any woman, at some level, and that, similarly, there is something indispensably male about any man. At the most fundamental level, this difference is so absolute, that the existence of two separate, distinct species of human being, one male and one female, exists in their minds.

To put it another way, one that is exceptionally unfashionable at the moment, men *do* subscribe to a sexual double standard. They *do* believe that the experience of human sexuality—genital intercourse in particular—is an inexpressibly powerful one, that it has a deep, perhaps fathomless impact on an individual's psychology. Since sexuality is so radically different an experience for a man and a woman, they contend that it is of indelible significance in the development of gender. Anatomy may not be destiny, but neither is it utterly discountable. In one form or another, every individual we interviewed, male or female, expressed this same point of view when asked to comment on the nature of the differences between masculinity and femininity. For example:

> I feel that for a man to say there's no such thing as a double standard is to deny that there is some basic, profound, fundamental biological difference between men and women. To me it keeps coming back to the fact that—at least it's a fact to me—that men have a different basis for their sexuality, a different experience of sexual love. Psychologically, at some rational level, men and women may be identical, but the physical experience (which is actually as much psychological as physical) is indisputable and powerful.
>
> It has something to do with woman being the receptor, the receiver in the physical sense, and with her being the one who is impregnated, who

has that role. Somehow nature has arranged it so that one sex is the bearer, and should have more protection, physically—is more like a vessel. That's putting it simplistically, maybe, but the point is that she cannot afford to be as free with herself, at some level. It's just a fact. Sexuality has to have more meaning to her. A man enters briefly into the picture, no matter what their relationship is. It's inborn with us. It makes a man's attitude, personality, sexuality different from hers, makes him less . . . makes *her* less casual.

I don't think that this will ever change. I don't think that sex will ever be truly as potentially inconsequential for a woman as it is, psychologically, for a man. Because women necessarily have that protective, inward feeling. . . .

Now to get a little more specific about men, I would have to say, if I were God and I was creating man and woman, I'd want my guy to fuck all the time to propagate the race. He would have to have that drive, he would have to be looking to do it all the time. It would take less to turn him on, and once he got turned on, he would *need* to do something about it, there would be a strong built-in drive to release the pressure of being aroused. He would be assertive about doing something about it. Hopefully, if you were going to do this gender thing with any intelligence, you would want men to be the sexual aggressors and you would want them to be very easily activated.

This doesn't necessarily mean—now, a lot of guys, and women too for that matter, make the mistake of thinking that this means that men have to naturally be polygamous. Not at all. It doesn't mean that at all. The fact that a male should have an easily aroused sex drive doesn't necessarily mean it has to be released with a lot of different women. One, ten thousand—the numbers aren't the point—it's that built-in, easily triggered arousal and the need to release it that has got to be there. And I think that's the way it is.

Another man put it this way:

> There's no doubt in my mind that there's some kind of transition going on, some sort of change in the way the sexes regard each other and relate to each other. Men are obviously becoming much more conscious of women as being something other than just attractive creatures that are pleasing to look at, to pursue, and to go to bed with. The men I know are trying to deal with women in a much friendlier way, trying to establish relationships with women where they can begin by relating as friends, where they can do things together as friends.
>
> I tend to assume that when you get right down to it most men are no different than I am. They try, as individuals, to avoid dealing with any situation from a preconceived point of view, from the point of view of some group identity, like "I'm a Republican, a Democrat, a sexist, a feminist," whatever. The men I know very definitely try to avoid "isms" of any kind. Those things don't have a lot of meaning to them. They're just extreme positions people take. Convenient labels. Actually, if you look at it carefully, you find that people who casually throw those kinds of labels around are just plain lazy. It's easier to categorize someone than to try to perceive his or her unique, individual qualities. . . .
>
> But the way in which I view the man-woman thing, I do see men and women as being basically different, categorically different. It may be because

of my hormones, I don't know, but there is a difference as far as I'm concerned, one that underlies the differences between individuals. It's at a deeper level altogether.

It's not something you have to constantly focus on—in a work situation I would expect the same thing from a woman that I would expect from a man. I make it a point in professional settings to react to a woman the same way that I react to a man. Actually, I think some women are confused by that, because men in business are generally fairly polite to other men—will hold doors open for them, reach across and unlock the car door, that kind of thing, and I've had women actually criticize me to my face for doing exactly those same things for them, as if it suddenly became sexist when you hold a door open for a woman, but it's just normal courtesy when you do it for a man.

At times, though, you learn that you're still being overly gracious with the ladies. For example, I play a lot of tennis, and I tend to be more restrained with a woman, since I just automatically tend to assume that they won't perform as well as a man, or at least I did until recently. So, for example, playing mixed doubles I would not tend to hit my serve as hard as I could to a woman, no matter what her level of proficiency was. But then I was in California not too long ago and played one of the best female tennis players I've ever played. I had to work not to get too badly beaten by her, and I was trying to win every point on my serve I could. So I'm still learning, like most men, I suppose.

Once clarification of the open-ended nature of this question was forthcoming, the responses of the women we spoke with tended to cautiously coincide with the male viewpoint set forth above. One thirty-seven-year-old Seattle nurse practitioner offered these thoughts on the nature of masculinity and femininity:

> If there's a difference between male and female sexuality and gender identity on the psychological level, I think it's based on the fact that women can get pregnant. There's no foolproof method of contraception yet, and it's always going to be the woman who suffers the consequences if her method doesn't work.
>
> I've had two abortions and they've unquestionably had a strong effect on me psychologically, particularly in the way I related to sex and to men afterwards, but in other ways too. I don't know how you can generalize from my particular situation, but the first time I had an abortion it was—I mean, the pregnancy was completely unexpected. I never thought I would get pregnant, until I did, and I never dreamed I would have an abortion. I just didn't think about it. In fact, I always wanted to have kids. I was twenty-three, and it was harder to get an abortion then, but not impossible. But the man I got pregnant by I only slept with once. He had just left a long-term relationship with someone else, and he made it clear right away that he didn't want to get involved again in a heavy relationship with anyone. He wanted to keep it casual, sleep with other women, all that sort of thing. In fact, what he said was that even though he liked what was happening between us, it had the feeling of a long-term relationship from the start, so he thought we should cool it, that I should back off a little.
>
> Well, I *was* becoming emotionally attached to him, and I *was* hoping it would become more serious as time went on, so when he said that, it

was like a cold bath. It hurt my feelings so much that I did a complete about-face—you know, wounded pride and all that—and when I found out I was pregnant, I thought, "I'll be damned if I'll tell him about it and ask him to help me." So I wasn't seeing him at all anymore, and I just kind of crawled off by myself like some kind of wounded animal and worked out all the abortion arrangements by myself.

But I had to go to Mexico with a couple of other women and all in all it was a pretty grim experience. It changed me. I think it's a lot like having a miscarriage. It takes a long time for your body to recover—at least it did for me. It's depressing to have something ripped out of your body. Actually it took me a total of about two years to really get over it, and all that time I basically felt angry and exploited. The second time I had an abortion was much better. It was in a feminist clinic here in Seattle and there was an incredibly strong sense of compassion and mutual supportiveness among all the women there, staff and patients alike. But I still think it's a sobering experience, and from my point of view I think that's where men and women are radically different, where their relationship to their own sexuality has to diverge.

The existence of this special kind of "double standard" in the minds of both men and women about the nature of their sexual differences does not in any way imply the continuation of a conventional, discriminatory double standard in all realms of social, economic, and political life. It simply means that one of the most significant interpersonal experiences of human existence can never be identical for men and women.

This point is worth emphasizing. As far as we can tell, there is nothing deterministic about this conviction in the minds of most men. They do not inevitably associate sexual differences with discriminatory gender stereotypes, such as those that repressively portray all women as soft, compliant, passive, and ultimately inferior or subordinate to men. Nor do they necessarily conclude that the existence of these sexual differences implies any sort of natural justification for institutionalized discrimination against women.

> My feeling is that the difference between the sexes is a powerful one, not only really powerful on what you might call the biological level, in terms of nature, but also on the more social level. It's something—it's a difference we can't overlook, but there are a lot of situations in daily life that do not have to be and should not have to be ruled by basic distinctions between the sexes.
> Where that dividing line is is probably pretty fuzzy a lot of the time, and that's what the women's movement seems to be saying: "Let's not make this sex difference thing a bigger deal than it has to be, let's readjust so that it doesn't have the effect of holding women back unnecessarily."
> That's fine, they're right. But on the other hand, biology isn't just a matter of lungs, muscles, cells, and genitals. It has a lot to do with attitude and that's not something we can afford to overlook either. It's something we tend to forget, to ignore, and we should pay more attention to it . . .
> I guess we're beginning to now. But when it comes to most social roles, the differences, the biological differences, they're no longer quite the point. I don't think just because women are sexually receptive that we should typecast them as having to have softer, yielding, more passive personalities, and so on all the way down the line. In fact it may be just the opposite, and in my experience it often is. Some women I know in business, when they put on their executive hat,

watch out, they're just as tough as any guys I've ever worked with, maybe a little more so. There've been cases in my business, in my career, where being a friend to a powerful woman in a business situation has definitely worked against me, because in her zeal to be fair and just, she will leave me out in the cold, *because* I'm a friend and she feels she can't afford to be called on showing favoritism. Now that's something that probably wouldn't happen in the "old boys network," where favoritism is the name of the game.

Furthermore, most of the men and women we talked to readily agreed that the traditional understanding of "masculine" and "feminine" roles may very well no longer be appropriate. Technological advances, particularly in the form of better contraception, labor-saving household appliances, and the dramatic reduction of the type and number of jobs that require sheer physical strength and stamina, have preconditioned most Americans to tolerate and even welcome changes in their expectations of male and female roles. Such recent cultural trends as concern over population growth and heightened sensitivity to individual civil rights among religious, ethnic, and other minorities, contribute to the climate of acceptance.

But our subjects also feel strongly that the evolution of these roles into an equitable social system will be a very long one, and that any form of gender equality must be predicated on a clear acknowledgment of gender differences. On balance, our respondents felt the statistical representation of the "average" man or the "average" woman consistently reveals significant differences in traits, skills, aptitudes, and affinities. Many women may indeed quite profitably become more "masculine," as the word is traditionally understood, and many men may well benefit from the cultivation of more traditionally "feminine" traits. According to these men and women, however, rearrangement of the traditional gender characteristics should not be misconstrued as the elimination of a fundamental difference between the sexes.

Despite a strong conviction among most men and many women that gender differentiation is more significant than has often been conceded in recent years, we sensed that there is also widespread confusion and a general lack of information about the extent of our understanding of gender distinctions. It might be worthwhile to mention a few of them, those that are universally accepted by scientific investigators.

The basis of gender is, of course, our natural physiological divison into two complementary sexes. The physiological differentiation between the sexes in terms of body size, shape, and musculature; skeletal and dental configuration; age of onset of puberty, and so on begins very early in life, in the embryo.

A number of researchers have recently concluded that the first and most basic substrata of all human sexual development is essentially female (i.e., the "Eve" principle). Only through the action, about six weeks after conception, of a very specific molecule, do embryos become "masculinized." Otherwise, all babies would be born female (for a few generations at least).

Regardless of its chromosome mix (XY for males; XX for females), the sexual development of an embryo is not fixed until after the first six weeks, at which time *most but not all* XY-chromosome embryos become male. Shortly afterward, at about twelve weeks after conception, *most* (but again *not all*) XX-chromosome embryos begin to develop as females. Occasionally a genetic female embryo develops male sexual features, and vice versa.

The action of the embryonic gonads strongly influences different brain development—specifically of the hypothalamus—in males and females. In the embryo, normal males acquire "masculinized" brains and normal females acquire "feminized" brains. Too much of the opposite sex hormone, or a failure on the part of the developing brain cells to respond properly to the appropriate hormone signals, can masculinize the brain of a female fetus or feminize the brain of a male fetus. In such cases, highly sex-specific patterns of neural interconnections, among other things, are altered.

Evidently, human neurological sexual differentiation implies different but by no means unequal kinds and areas of psychophysiological competence. Most scientists now accept the view that there are fundamental neurobiological differences between the way that the brains of men and women function, differences that strongly indicate that men and women do in fact think differently.

Recent brain research is one area where the influence of nature in dictating differences between the sexes appears to be undeniable. As neurobiologist Dr. Richard M. Restak observed in *The Brain: The Last Frontier,* many of the differences in brain function between men and women appear to be innate, biologically determined, and difficult or impossible to change by cultural influences.[14]

Restak points out that female infants have been shown to have significantly greater sensitivity at an earlier age to certain types of sounds, especially that of their mother's voice, than males. They also have greater tactile sensitivity than males, especially in their fingertips. Females generally are able to discriminate among various visual and auditory stimuli in their environments in order to identify a mother's face sooner than males can.

Males and females excel at different types of motor coordination skills: Men are better at overall body activity and have faster reaction times, but women are superior at finer tasks.

Males tend to be better at what are usually called "visual-spatial" tasks, such as mentally folding or rotating a three-dimensional object, or finding their way through an imaginary maze. Females excel at verbal tasks, especially at language acquisition and mastery. Men's brains appear to be more "compartmentalized" than women's, with the right-hand hemisphere tending to be exclusively dominated by nonverbal and the left by verbal functions.

Finally, some researchers draw a distinction between the way female and male infants tend to learn about their environment. Males, they claim, tend to be more curious and to depend more heavily on active exploration and manipulation of what they encounter around them. Perceiving a blinking light, they are more likely than females to try to approach and disassemble it.

Females, according to this viewpoint, tend to have a more "communicative" mode of learning about their surroundings than males. They ask questions, watch for social cues, and are more likely to conform to observable social norms. They tend also to possess greater interpersonal skills and greater sensitivity to even very subtle modulations of voice and facial expression.

On the other hand, none of these inherent distinctions necessarily implies the continuation of what we have come to think of in this last decade or so as traditional masculine and feminine traits. Restak, for example, is careful to also cite the findings of a Stanford University study by Eleanor Maccoby and Carol Nagby Jacklin, who found that "intellectual performance is incompatible with our stereotype of femininity in girls or masculinity in boys. Recent studies even suggest that high levels of intellectual achievement call for cross-sex typing: the ability to express traits and interests associated with the opposite sex."[15]

It is important to understand that these generalizations about men and women are just that: generalizations. Few of the studies on infants are so conclusive that they cannot be disagreed with, and most have been disputed. Our understanding of the neurobiological foundations of gender is itself in its infancy, as is our understanding of precisely how gender informs adult behavior. Furthermore, it is also plainly true that as men and women grow from infancy to adulthood, it becomes more and more difficult to distinguish between behavior that is biologically engendered and that which is predominantly the result of socialization.

Unfortunately, the preponderant stance in recent years toward the biological dimensions of gender on the part of gender activists has tended to be a biased rather than evenhanded one. Perhaps in reaction to the work of anthropologists and ethnologists like Konrad Lorenz *(On Aggression)* and Lionel Tiger *(Men in Groups),* there has appeared among gender liberals an irrational tendency to cast "nature" and "nurture" into antithetical positions. This leads to the contention that the only hope for a truly just and equitable future for women lies in a concentration on nurture, at the risk of displacing nature.

> Human beings are radically distinguished from all other animals by their freedom from instinctual determination. We have less instinctual knowledge than baboons when we are born, but our capacity for varying responses is infinitely greater. Self-consciousness, the need for self-esteem, and the ability to create and manipulate complex symbolic systems—found only in humans and made possible by a uniquely large neocortex—allow human beings to ascribe a wide range of different meanings to the same event and to act accordingly. Animals do not measure their activities against a conscious internal ideal; they may defend their young, but they will not die for an idea, a country, or to prove to themselves that they are qualified members of their sex.[16]
>
> —Marc Feigen Fasteau

The prevailing scientific view is a relatively unassuming and commonsensical one. Nature and nurture, it submits, work in tandem, contributing interdependently to the process by which individuals of both sexes mature into the full realization of their gender potential.

> Gender identity in adulthood is the end product not of an either-or determinism of heredity versus environment, but of the genetic code in serial interaction with the environment. From the time of conception, the genetic code unfolds itself in interaction, first with the intrauterine environment, then the perinatal environment, the family environment, and eventually the more extended

social, biological, and inanimate ecological environment. Interactionism is a key principle, but an even more basic key is the principle of serial sequence of interaction.[18]

—John Money

When we asked the men we interviewed if they could elaborate a bit on what they felt to be the elements of masculinity as they understood it, we ran into problems. Though they upheld the existence of gender differentiation, they were by and large unable to do more than sketch out in a very impressionistic manner what they believe to be the exact nature of the distinction:

> It may be somewhat different for every person in the world, but I guess for me being feminine means being receptive; being masculine means being staunch.
> A feminine tree would be like a willow tree, the wind would blow and it would sort of bend with the wind. Very accommodating. It would take an incredibly strong wind to actually break the tree because it would be able to bend so much with whatever was happening.
> A masculine tree would be something like an oak, a tree that would just stand there in the face of whatever was coming at it. The oak would be very strong, stronger than the willow in many ways, but it would probably break before the willow, just be knocked clean over because it lacked resilience.

Another respondent offered this comment:

> At some levels, men and women are the same, psychologically. In the sense that everyone has to become a strong, self-assured, and in that sense

powerful person who knows himself or herself and knows what his or her life is all about, in that sense, we're all the same.

But how we go about that, I see it more in terms of balances of different kinds of energies rather than in rigid stereotypes. Yin energy and yang energy. A woman is basically yin energy with some yang, and a man is basically yang energy, with some yin. But that doesn't mean a particular woman couldn't be more yang than yin, or a particular man couldn't be more yin than yang, could have more feminine energy in that sense. I suppose it could even work out that in some couples the woman could be the provider and the man could stay home. In theory that could work very well for some people and in fact now that I think about it, I'm sure that there are couples who do it that way. For me it wouldn't, though.

Another way to look at it is based on the fact that a woman has a different body than a man. That's not some kind of oppressive head trip about a woman has to behave this way, or that way. It's more like, if a woman is living with a sense of harmony with her body and a man is living with a sense of harmony with his body, there is going to be a difference between the two of them. Man has a more definite, angular body, and his relationship to the world tends to be more hard-edged, you could say, in certain ways. If a woman feels her femininity as a woman, even a perfectly strong, self-reliant woman, then it seems like her body is softer and she has a more well-rounded perspective on it, to use a pretty metaphorical way of describing it. I think that's the best I can do.

Although I very definitely like *strong* women, I do not like *hard* women. There's an important difference to me. It's like a woman who is too hard-edged is too strident, is denying one aspect of feminine energy. It's almost like they have to be aggressively masculine, as overcompensation for being feminine at all. There's no reason to deny it, as if the feminine was an ugly or crumby part of themselves.

Most men were readier to offer criticisms of the traditional masculine ethos, particularly to its insensitive, detached, unemotional overemphasis on logic and objectivity, than to try to analyze masculinity's positive attributes:

Too many men are completely overwhelmed by their rationality. Very reason oriented, very knowledgeable, but not much intuition or wisdom about themselves. The most important thing is missing: understanding of oneself as a human being, psychologically, emotionally, and maybe even physically.

Other respondents pointed to a masculine propensity, based on preoccupation with the sexual gratification that the female body represents to them, to become so fixated on the differences between the sexes that they entirely overlook the important human commonalities that men and women share. In other words, many of the men we spoke to made a point of criticizing the tendency of their own sex to dehumanize women by treating them in an impersonal way, as sex objects, often to the exclusion of all other considerations and kinds of interactions. The masculine tendency to believe in a natural, immutable distinction between the sexes, they felt, does often stray perilously close to a kind of gender xenophobia. Since women are viewed as mysteriously and alluringly different, they are also seen as alien, and are ultimately mistrusted. One man described to us with singular drama the vivid moment when he realized in more than just a conceptual way that women are human beings too:

I remember, vividly, the exact moment—literally—when I first realized that women are, underneath it all, more like me than I used to think. I was at a party, four or five years ago, at my girlfriend's house. We were all sitting around, maybe eight people, after dinner in the living room, just talking. One woman, a friend of Dorothy's, her name was Arlene I think, was describing something, some experience she had been through—it's probably irrelevant just what it was she was talking about—and as I watched her, and listened to her, it dawned on me . . . I suddenly had the absolutely astonishing experience, for the first time in my life—and I'm by no means an insensitive, uncompassionate person, I mean I have always thought of myself as really having an imagination, or really being able to empathize with other people's experiences—of really, truly, honestly, totally, completely understanding that at some level, underneath the irrefutable differences that do exist between men and women, we really are in many ways the same damn creature. It was literally a relevation to me. I was dumbfounded . . . thunderstruck. It was like suddenly, in a flash of intuitive insight, understanding the theory of relativity. I knew, in an instant's perception, that men and women were, at some level, a lot more similar than I had ever, ever dreamed before . . . That, let me tell you, was an experience I have never forgotten. It completely changed my perspectives on women, and my life.

In general, we noticed that the attempts of these men to define masculinity could be assigned to three different categories: positive, negative, and ambivalent.

In the first, the plus category, fell most of their references to masculine courage and masculine willingness to assume major, lifelong responsibilities, primarily those associated with work and family. In the second category, as we saw in the interview extract above, fell most masculine discussions of the alienation of men from their feelings. The men we spoke to almost unanimously agreed with the conventional view that many men have overdeveloped their analytical faculties at the expense of their emotional, intuitive, and esthetic sensibilities.

In the middle, in the category that our respondents expressed the most ambivalent feelings about, appeared a constellation of qualities and traits that centered on masculine competitiveness, which most men believe to be essential to success in the economic marketplace, but which they are also well aware can lead an individual to become excessively ambitious, driven, and in some cases dangerously overstressed.

Finally, it seems worth noting that any view that predicates two fundamentally distinct sorts of psychosexual experience in human beings has unavoidable implications for the alternative of androgyny, often articulated by more visionary gender activists. Unfortunately, their articulation has to date been an elusively piecemeal and ambiguous one. If the vision is of a society in which the terms "masculine" and "feminine" no longer have any meaning, a society in which the attitudes and behavior of men and women are deliberately, methodically restructured to eradicate any hint of sexual differentiation beyond the biological level, then we think the prospects of an "androgynous" society are unfavorable and its advocates quixotic. As one of our participants succinctly put it, "Androgyny? What does that really mean. I hear that word used a lot, but no one seems to really know what it means. If it means some kind of sexual neutering, forget it!"

On the other hand, if it is instead, a vision of a society in which men and women will be free to identify, explore, and integrate personality traits they may have had to repress out of exaggerated fears of being thought "too masculine" or "too feminine," then we have no doubt most men will sanction its development.

> Perhaps in the future, our lives will be shaped by a view of personality which will not assign fixed ways of behaving to individuals on the basis of sex. Instead, it would acknowledge that each person has the potential to be—depending on the circumstances—both assertive *and* yielding, independent *and* dependent, job *and* people oriented, strong *and* gentle, in short both "masculine" and "feminine"; that the most effective and happy individuals are likely to be those who have accepted and developed both these "sides" of themselves; and that to deny either is to mutilate and deform; that human beings, in other words, are naturally adrogynous.[19]
>
> —Marc Feigen Fasteau

• *These men impressed us as being far more monogamous than the traditional male stereotype acknowledges.*

After a brief period of being considered archaic, monogamous values appear to be reasserting themselves strongly in men's (and women's) attitudes toward their relationships. Despite the categorical—and in our opinion unfounded—assertions of those like Phyllis Chesler, author of *Women and Madness*, who are prepared to insist that "few men are committed to the ethic of love or sexual monogamy,"[20] a strong majority of the men we talked to voiced an unequivocal desire either to find a woman with whom they could establish a deep and, ideally, lasting monogamous attachment, or to maintain that level of commitment if they were already involved in such a relationship. None of the men that we spoke to expressed any desire for an unattached, polygamous lifestyle.

> I'd like to settle down in a one-to-one relationship, and I'm looking forward to getting married again. But it's difficult to find a woman who already

knows herself really well, and who is compatible with me. . . .

I think people shy away from monogamous commitments because they're afraid. They think, "Oh my God, what am I getting into?" There's a panic about getting trapped with the wrong person and then having to adjust or admit how much you dislike being with him or her. But it's gotten to a point in my own life where I've finally—here I am, forty-two, it's taken me a long time—come to terms with that panic in such a way that I know it isn't going to louse up a really good relationship when and if I get involved with one.

But for most men *and* women that panic is a very strong thing: "What am I getting into?," they think. I find that in a way the tables are turned these days. Most men I know would like nothing better than to really settle down, really make that commitment, and then really work to make it work out once they do. But most women I meet make it clear, at least to me, that they really aren't willing to get involved in a deep relationship, which to me is really odd, because when you get to know them well enough to ask how they feel about all these fleeting, obviously superficial sexual connections they make with men, they always say, "Yechh!" and act like that's really a dissatisfying lifestyle for them.

Even the few men under thirty-five-years-old that we interviewed held what we judged to be a basically monogamous perspective about their relationships. Said one, for example:

I haven't been able to find a woman that I relate to well in terms of being close friends and lovers with and who then also wants to further the relationship, to delve deeper into it, to form a commitment between the two of us. In most cases, they back out, sabotage it, or close up emotionally somehow. They end it. It's strange. It almost seems like they're afraid.

Another man, a twenty-eight-year-old assistant branch manager for a large West Coast savings and loan organization, concurred:

> I'm finding out now that I just don't meet many women who are ready to be heavily involved in a one-to-one relationship. They don't want to get tied down, and they don't want you to have any expectations about the relationship at all. A woman may very well spend the night with me, then when I call up the next day, just to say something casual and friendly like, "Hi, I really enjoyed your company," she'll freak out. She'll immediately say something like, "Look, I like you too, but let's keep it light and casual. Don't take it too seriously. I'm just not interested in getting heavily involved with anyone right now."
>
> From my point of view, women these days are where men were ten years ago. They want to keep everything on a superficial, noncommital level.
>
> Either that or I find that the women I meet that I feel some real rapport with are already taken, they are already seriously involved in a relationship with someone else. Just that fact alone—that there are so many women around who are *not* available—makes me suspect there's a lot more monogamy in men than most of us have been willing to admit.
>
> I guess I'm just looking for someone, hoping to run into someone, who is a very open, creative,

totally alive woman. Looking for that with my whole being. It's quite frustrating actually.

The stereotypical notion of the male as an unreliable philanderer is not an especially pleasing one to most thoughtful, sensitive men. There is no doubt in our minds that the men we spoke to, for example, would be only too happy to be free of the minor but annoying repercussions they've encountered throughout their lives from this conventional image of the male as a kind of hapless sexual delinquent.

> Frankly, I feel like, you know, who needs it? That subtle peer pressure to make suggestive comments about passing women, the whole jealousy and distrust bit that you automatically get from wives. I've even had job interviewers just flat out tell me that they prefer not to hire single men—which is against the law, of course—because they're "not as stable" as married men, meaning that they screw around more I guess. Anyway, most of the men I know think the whole "man the lecher" bit is pretty silly. . . .
> I can kind of see how the image gets started, though. I mean, I used to think the average male would happily fuck warm mud, and that's about all he cared about, that he was functioning at that level of discrimination. But now I look at it differently. I think that's a dehumanizing way to look at men, and a self-destructive way for men to look at themselves.
> I think what that attitude tends to overlook is that most men are just now beginning to realize that they are as interested in women as companions as they are in sex, in women as lovers. The oversexed aspect of the masculine image is mostly hype, if you ask me. I think it's just something for

insecure men to hang their identities on. Not that good sex isn't a great thing alright, but most men want someone they count on as a friend, as a partner—all those other things that a good complete relationship with someone makes possible. . . .

There's an enormous amount of sexual hype in this country, particularly in the media. As much as anything else, that's what contributes to the kind of sexual agitation and restlessness that you get among so many people, men and women, these days. They're bombarded by images and sounds and words that are calculated to get them overheated, but most of them have enough sense to more or less shrug it off. Sure they're going to fantasize about other lovers no matter what kind of commitment they have to their current relationship—that's entirely human, entirely natural, entirely inevitable—but very few feel like they have to act on it, at least among the men and women I know. Not if it means jeopardizing a good relationship, and in most cases, that's exactly what it would mean. . . . For me, my marriage is like a fine tool. If it's well made, I can take it and use it to create nearly anything my imagination can conceive of. And so can my wife. It takes teamwork, which is often a very satisfying experience in and of itself, and you don't always know where you'll wind up in the end, like with having kids, but just the fact of knowing that the tool is there is enormously satisfying to me . . . I think the opposite of what I'm talking about would be the idea of marriage as some kind of experimental situation—you know, "Well let's get married and try it out and see how it goes. No big deal, if it doesn't work out, we'll just get a divorce." Test-tube marriages. It's an idea that's been popular for the last ten, twenty years, but I don't think that's how real marriages work. Without a basic agreement to try to stick to the relationship come hell or high water, you haven't got that basic tool, and you can't make anything really happen. Eventually you start to wonder why you're even together with this other person.

Oddly enough, even on the rare occasions when it is conceded that the average man may indeed be more monogamous than he has usually been portrayed, there often lingers the insinuation that his monogamy is of a basically negative, defensive, and selfish type. His desire to form a close, monogamous relationship with a woman is seen as stemming from essentially self-protective, pragmatic motivations: He wants a source of respite from occupational pressures; he expects her to function as a housekeeper for him.* He is unconsciously seeking to recreate the sense of appreciation and security he enjoyed as a child cared for and protected by his mother. More recently, the charge is that because the emergent sexual assertiveness and independence of liberated women threatens him, and because he has found he dislikes having no sexual claim on the women he becomes attached to more than he dislikes having to restrict his own sexual freedom, a monogamous arrangement is the lesser of two evils.

There may be an element of truth in such allegations, but we believe our interview extracts demonstrate that there is also an equally valid and much more positive interpretation of the masculine propensity to seek monogamous arrangements with women. First, we found that men who were not already engaged in a monogamous sexual union, strongly and we felt sin-

---

*It is not that men do not love and care for their wives. They do, but only in the context of the *traditional marriage,* a relationship structured to preserve the husband's sense of being different from and superior to his wife, to allow him, if he is an upper-middle-income professional, to pursue the kind of total commitment to career expected of him, to pressure his wife into living her life through and around his career and the friends he makes through his work.[21]
—Marc Feigen Fasteau

cerely, desired one because they believed *both* partners would benefit. Second, we noticed that men who felt they had already found the appropriate partner for such a relationship voiced no regrets whatsoever about terminating any simultaneous relationships they may have been pursuing. In fact, as far as we could determine from their recollections in their conversations with us, most of these men had felt distinctly relieved finally to have found themselves in a position where they could wholeheartedly focus all their time, energy, and affection on one person. Finally, and most important, we sense that many of the men we spoke with understand and profoundly appreciate what has been referred to as the "binding magic of intimacy." They know that a certain type of initial sexual attraction is ultimately transient. It wears off. And they also know that it is replaced by the absurd and wonderful miracle of being liked in spite of the fact that one's partner has seen through the public facade to the private and often unimpressive self. They know, in short, that "intimacy" occurs because the initial images of both individuals in the pair eventually fade away, yet in spite of this disenchantment, each partner still genuinely likes and supports the other. As one man recounted:

> I remember, having been married only about two years at the time, suddenly one day thinking, "My wife actually likes me." Then it struck me how strange a thought that was. I realized that what I meant was that she likes me even though she now knows the real me, the private me who is not the genius the public is supposed to see. Until then I could never understand how old people stayed together. I guess that was when I understood the actual friendship and real mutual affection that rises out of that intense initial male-female attraction.

It is also true, however, that even the most intense masculine appetite for a monogamous relationship is not without its

ambivalence, much of which is just a particularized expression of the classical, general male ambivalence about women.*
Compelled by his intense desire for intimate and lasting sexual involvement with a woman,† a man may at first be delighted to find himself involved in the stable, captivating relationship he has longed for. But the very fulfillment of longstanding and insistent desires for sexual acceptance and gratification can evoke deep-seated fears of becoming too open, too vulnerable, and the risk of painful depression should the relationship fail. Thus, self-protective mechanisms of emotional detachment are involuntarily activated. The net effect in both sexes is a classic approach-avoidance conflict, a double-bind with all its attendant anxiety, frustration, depression, and anger.

By making the value of autonomy so fundamental to the achievement of its goal, the women's movement has had the effect of encouraging women to leave relationships in which they are excessively dependent, and to avoid making new commitments prematurely. This is an invaluable achievement. At the same time, it has intensified anxiety in men. Of those men we talked to who were married or otherwise significantly involved with independent women who were busy pursuing careers of their own, most (about three-quarters) admitted to having had to cope at some point with deep-seated fears that her increasing independence and economic self-sufficiency, combined with her increasing contact with other men in the occupational marketplace, would lead her to become dissatisfied with him and would eventually encourage her to leave the relationship. In other words, as humiliating as it is for many men to confess to helplessness or anxieties of other than a superficial kind, most of those men we spoke to candidly

---

*The history of misogyny has been abundantly documented by Hoffman R. Hays and Wolfgang Lederer, M.D., as well as meticulously investigated from a psychoanalytic viewpoint by, among others, Dorothy Dinnerstein.[22]
†After spending a year working as a columnist for a men's magazine, during which she received descriptions of their sexual fantasies from more than 3,000 men, author Nancy Friday has been quoted as concluding that "men want women more than women want men."[23]

acknowledged significant personal difficulty in overcoming an automatic association of the economic advancement of women with fears of being criticized, rejected, and possibly also ultimately abandoned by their female partners.

> My wife is an executive headhunter and she travels all over the country . . . primarily in the Southeast, but she goes all over. She's been with her present employer five years now, and it's only built up gradually, her having to travel so much, but I remember her first trip vividly, how much it really got to me. She's going to Boston next week, and I'll be going along with her on this trip, but that's unusual. The first time she had to travel, my head really got turned around. I had to work on it for awhile to get things straight within myself, to feel honestly comfortable about it.
>
> We knew it was coming, that first time, and so it wasn't really any kind of a surprise at all, but when the guy came and picked her up in the company car, and she carried her suitcase out the front door and tossed it in the back, and climbed in and away they went, it was . . . I stood in the doorway for a long time. I guess I felt, oh, a little like we were going in opposite directions.
>
> Anyway, we did a lot of talking about it and I'm much more comfortable with the situation now. She's a very strong woman, and she held fast to what she felt and what she believed in, what she knew in her gut was right for her. She understood how sensitive I felt at first about her being out in the totally male world of business, but she wasn't about to give it up.
>
> It was the right thing for her to do, too. I had to change *my* attitudes, and I did. It worked. She held her ground, I changed my point of view, and we had a lot to talk about about trust and sexuality

and people in general and how they are. I'm sure I'm not unlike other males in that your wife never screws around with some ugly son of a gun . . . they're always, at least in your fantasies, really great looking guys, and wealthier and smarter than you to boot. As soon as I got it straight in my head that *I* was okay, that she wasn't trying to get away from me, and that she was just doing what she really wanted and needed to do with her life, it eased that pain for me for awhile.

Herb Goldberg describes the male dilemma over monogamy in related but slightly different terms. Under a section captioned "Sexual Stereotypes and Myths" in *The New Male,* he makes these comments about the assumption that men are not basically monogamous:

> I believe that the conditioning of the male creates in him a powerful ambivalence toward monogamy. On the one hand, he has a deep craving for a special female partner based on his early experience of mother as his lifeline and source of nourishment and comfort. This is coupled with other factors that cause him to hunger for one special partner, such as his intense emotional isolation from other men because of his competitive stance toward them, his fear of being open and vulnerable in front of them, his homosexual anxiety and the fact that men are not usually sources of nourishment and comfort to each other. Finally, his orientation toward "his" woman is usually a possessive, protective, and guilt-laden one. All of these factors tend to make him lean *toward* monogamy.
>
> His push *away* from monogamy would result from early conditioning in which he learned to view sex as a game of challenge and conquest. His

masculinity was validated by the number of women who would go to bed with him. Second, his emotional and sensual repression and a concomitant tendency to relate to sex in terms of goal (ejaculation) rather than process (the pleasure of sexual play) would tend to create boredom and rigidity with any partner. Third, if his wife or lover is the traditional reactive-passive-submissive woman sexually, she will be a monotonous, highly predictable partner and will also trigger his tendency to feel guilty and self-hating for feelings of imposing himself on her. Finally, unconscious resentment over the strictures of his role may reflect itself in sexual resistance. All of this would tend to pull him *away* from monogamy.

In general, powerful ambivalence rather than a clear-cut positive or negative feeling would seem to be the logical experience of the traditional man.[24]

Though Goldberg's view of the masculine conflict over monogamy strikes us as having, on balance, an excessively negative cast, our conversations with these men appeared to corroborate certain elements of Goldberg's argument. His implication is that much of the philandering behavior, traditionally alluded to as evidence of a fundamentally polygamous predilection in men, is, in fact, symptomatic of sexual compulsiveness, repression, and just plain boredom. In other words, it seems to us that the traditional masculine irritation with the strictures of monogamy may with equal validity be interpreted as arising from a failure to realize fully the satisfactions that monogamous relationships have the potential to offer as from any sort of inherent male predisposition for sexual promiscuity.

In our interviews we noticed that men's own explanations of masculine infidelity in monogamous relationships tended to fall into one of the three generic categories, each of which was entirely compatible—in an inverted sort of way—with our postulation of a fundamentally monogamous masculine sexual orientation. First, many male adulterers, according to our interview participants, are simply conforming to that male role model that reacts more or less impetuously to what it considers to be the "challenge" posed by every ostensibly available woman. Marc Feigen Fasteau was, we believe, one of the first gender writers to label this a "sex as conquest" orientation, one that "makes men feel obliged to make some show of sexual interest in every attractive woman they see, some movement toward putting their stamp on her, whether or not they are in fact drawn to her."[25]

The pathology of this particular sexual orientation that is most self-evident is its compulsiveness. Since it is a function of need for constant reconfirmation of the masculinity of a specific individual, it tends to follow a neurotically repetitive, self-limiting pattern. Once the current object of attention has been sexually "conquered," her function as a foil for the demonstration of his virility is by definition ended. He then rapidly loses interest in her, and begins again, often blatantly, to resume his quest for sexual "challenge."

As self-centered as these men often readily concede their behavior to be, they are also often quick to point out that they do not intend by it, nor do they experience, any significant degree of disengagement from or violation of their commitment to a primary relationship. Their view of these secondary conquests tends to be unapologetically hypocritical: They see male infidelity as a trivial—if highly pleasurable—pastime.

That a conventional double standard in terms of marital infidelity still prevails in many parts of the country has been recently confirmed by meticulous research. In a study of the extramarital sexual experiences of 205 recently separated or divorced men and women, Professors Graham B. Spanier and Randie Margolis of Pennsylvania State University report that:

> ... thirty-four percent of the males and fifty-nine percent of the females reported that they felt either somewhat or very guilty after engaging in

extramarital sex. This suggests that a large number of respondents do not deem extramarital relationships appropriate even with the existence of marital problems. Many individuals may accept the common assumption that extramarital sex is "wrong" under all conditions, and would feel guilty for engaging in extramarital sex no matter what precipitated its occurrence. *A significantly higher percentage of males (forty-six percent) reported feeling no guilt for engaging in extramarital sex. This may suggest a double standard in terms of which gender is allowed to have an extramarital relationship without experiencing guilt. Men may feel that an extramarital relationship is appropriate if they choose to engage in one, and not experience as much guilt as women.*[26] [Italics ours.]

However, it also appears from the results of this study that the double standard is far less clearcut than it was only thirty years ago. Whereas Kinsey found that approximately twice as many men as women have had extramarital sex, Spanier and Margolis found that "thirty-eight percent of the males and thirty-seven percent of the females in the sample stated that they had engaged in extramarital sex."[27] In support of our contention that male infidelity does not necessarily indicate the absence of a basically monogamous behavior pattern, Spanier and Margolis note that "It appears that most of the extramarital relations occurred at a time when marriages presumably were expected to continue," and that "sixty-two percent of all respondents who engaged in extramarital sex reported either that their last extramarital affair had some emotional commitment or was a more long-term love relationship. This suggests that even if these relationships began fortuitously, many of them were perceived to have developed into emotional, caring relationships. Furthermore, this result precludes the idea that sexual satisfaction alone maintains the majority of extramarital relationships. For the majority of the respondents who engaged in extramarital sex, much more than just sex usually was involved in the relationship," and finally that "seventy percent of the respondents who engaged in extramarital sex reported that their extramarital relations were a result of marital problems."[28]

In other words, the results of this study support the view that infidelity for many men and women is a derivative phenomenon, one that reflects the inadequacy of the primary monogamous relationship and the powerful underlying drive to replace it with another, ideally better relationship, but one which is also essentially monogamous. The pattern suggested by this study is *not* one of concurrent, equally significant, polygamous involvements.

However, the casual duplicity of some men in regard to their affairs does not always extend to women: infidelities on the part of their wives, whether real or imagined, often precipitates violent psychological trauma in men.

> I remember a man I used to work with had this laissez-faire attitude about his affairs. Was very blatant about them, chased most of the women in the office at one time or another, until it got to be kind of an office joke—I mean no one ever really took Harv seriously after awhile. But still, every once in awhile there'd be a Christmas party or something and you'd meet his wife and she seemed like a completely decent person and you'd have to wonder how she could tolerate it. I mean, you'd have to ask yourself, What is it, do they have an open marriage, you know, is she out there carrying on with men just as much as he is with women? But people in the office who knew them a little better than I did were always saying, No, no, she's just a normal person, really good-hearted, and Harv is just what he seems like, a two-timing jerk, and it's really hard on her because she knows what's going on and she always has to make excuses

for him and try to pretend that things are alright between them.

Well, it went on like that for years, literally. I came to work here in 1967 and it was still going on in 1976. Nine years at least that I know about, probably more. Then one day Harv didn't show up at work. No big deal, no one even said anything about it to me for a couple of days and then I heard someone say they thought he had the flu. He was out for quite awhile, maybe two-three weeks, and people wondered a little about it, because that's a long time to be out with the flu, but you know how it is, everyone is busy, overworked, and has their own problems to take care of, so they kind of let it slide and don't think too much about it.

O.K., so it had been, oh, I guess three weeks, maybe three and a half, somewhere in there, and still no one was paying any real attention to it, except to kind of imply that maybe Harv was really using up all his sick time as a kind of a vacation, but no one thought that there was anything wrong at all.

Then one day a big group, maybe six of us, came back from lunch one day and got off the elevator and Frank wandered off down the hall toward his office and the rest of us were standing around and we kind of notice Frank walk past Harv's office, do a kind of double take, back up, and lean in and say, "Hey Harv, where you been, how you doing?" that kind of thing. So we all walked down there and there he is, just sitting there, sitting at his desk, hands on his knees, sitting there, staring straight ahead at the wall, not saying a thing. We all crowded in, talked to him—*tried* to talk to him, but he just sat there, not saying a thing, not moving a muscle. Well of course some guys thought it was a joke at first, and really made asses out of themselves, saying things like, "What's wrong Harv, are they making you sit in the corner because you've been out so long?" Stupid things like that, you know. I'm glad it wasn't me. But after a while, it started to get spooky, and we don't quite believe he's faking it anymore.

So, to make a long story short, eventually we had to have an ambulance come and take him for observation, and he got committed. I think he's still there. A lot of the people at work were against it at first, calling a hospital, cause they were afraid it would look bad and ruin his career, but you know, after he'd been sitting there for an hour and a half and no one could get him to talk, or blink, or anything, we got worried, and besides, we thought if he knew that we were about to call an ambulance for him, and he was just faking, he'd snap out of it. Anyway, I guess the stigma of seeing a shrink was the least of his problems.

It turns out what had happened was that his wife had finally gotten completely fed up with him and gone off and had an affair of her own. But very brief, a day or two at the most, or so I heard later. I guess she got scared and called it off almost as soon as it got started, she was just so unused to doing anything like that, and she just couldn't get over feeling that it was basically wrong. And then she made the big mistake of telling Harv about it. She wanted to clear her conscience, confess to him, that kind of thing. Well, he flipped out. Went completely berserk. Tore the house up, beat her up, threw her out—literally—threatened her life, called up the other guy and threatened his life, just went nuts. She didn't want to call the cops so she went to stay with her sister, and then Harv showed up there and threatened her sister. It got really ugly. He seemed to calm down for awhile, but then she found out he was following her around in his car everywhere she went. Finally I guess she went to the cops, got a restraining order, something like that, and that was when he showed up at the office, and that was that. Later we heard that that day in the office he'd had a gun in his desk, in a drawer in the desk. Very spooky.

Our interview participants also referred to a second type of adulterer, one who is far less compulsive than the first. He commits infidelities only very rarely, in many instances somewhat absentmindedly, in moments of intense loneliness or in unusual circumstances involving unusual loss of normal inhibition. Afterwards, he invariably feels intense remorse, and is usually compelled to confess his lapse to his partner. In our opinion, it was clear to the men we talked to that this category of infidelity represents no fundamental deviation from a primarily monogamous sexual behavior pattern.

Finally, there were references to a third type, the "message" infidelity, one that signals deep dissatisfaction with the current relationship, one that virtually begs to be discovered. Message infidelities, these men felt, were often highly reliable precursors of the dissolution of the primary relationship. Only if the revealed infidelity was interpreted as a somewhat clumsy way of saying, "I'm bored and disappointed and I want something to change so that the excitement we once felt about each other can be recaptured," did the relationship stand a genuine chance of surviving in their opinion, provided of course it was actually reexamined and restructured so as to more fully meet each partner's needs.

Usually, however, in their experience the message had been more along the lines of, "It's over, I'm looking for a new partner, I just don't have the guts to tell you to your face." In these cases, understandably, most relationships soon terminated.

The message infidelity clearly poses the most serious threat to an ongoing primary relationship, but by the same token it also represents the most intense and even idealistic (if somewhat paradoxical) search for fulfillment of the monogamous ideal. Conceivably, men and women who choose this kind of escape from a primary commitment betray in the very act of selecting such an indirect means of departure the repressive extent and depth of their sense of obligation to the relationship, their intimidation by it, and the degrading effects of intense anxiety over failing to live up to it. Furthermore, as Spanier and Margolis pointed out, they often leave an established primary relationship only when they have succeeded in developing a second, competing liaison, one that they hope will become an even more rewarding experience of what is at bottom still essentially a highly monogamous quest. Relatively few of the men or women who engage in message infidelities do so simply because they want to be unattached: What they want is to be *reattached*, to a partner who looks better to them, for any one of a number of reasons.

Unfortunately, it appears that few of the new relationships that arise out of message infidelities last. As Spanier and Margolis observe, "seventy-three percent of all but the most recent extramarital relationships had ended by the time of the interview . . . In general, they do not lead to new relationships."[29]

As painful as any form of breach of trust can be for both partners in a primary relationship, it deserves reemphasis here that underlying each type of ostensible deviation from monogamy is a level of genuine, if somewhat displaced, allegiance to the monogamous ideal.

• *These men were much more appreciative of the conventional family than the traditional masculine stereotype leads one to expect.*

Hand in hand with the myth of man the polygamous sexual nomad goes the longstanding myth of man the reluctant—or at best indifferent—family man. More recently, the literature of gender radicalism has often taken an opposite but equally jaundiced view of the relationship between men and the family, portraying the family as nothing more than a patriarchal institution contrived by men to assure the supply of an inexpensive source of domestic labor, as well as an inexhaustible pool of breeding stock. In short, this is the reductive view of the family as a trap, one designed to keep women "barefoot and pregnant," confined to the bedroom, the nursery and the kitchen.

Both of these mutually contradictory stereotypes—man the anti-family gypsy and man the overbearing family patriarch— were refuted by the responses of the men we spoke to, by their level-headed assessments of the value and purpose of the family. All the men we talked with made a conventional distinction between the institutions of "family" and "marriage." Marriage to these men simply implied a consensual agreement between two adults, usually based on sexual interdependence, but which also commonly involves companionship and the sharing of domestic, financial, social, and other responsibilities. If the statements of these men are any measure, the institution of marriage is in excellent shape in this country. Without exception, every man we spoke with who wasn't already happily married expressed an unconditional desire to develop a relationship that could culminate in a marriage-like mutual commitment.*

---

*Others have pointed convincingly in recent years to the soundness of the institution of marriage, among them George Gilder and Jessie Bernard. Gilder notes that:

> While divorces are increasing, so are marriages, to the point that a higher proportion of our people get married now, at least once, than ever before.[5] [5: "Is the American Family in Danger?", U.S. News and World Report, April 16, 1973, p. 71]. The highest divorce rate, moreover, comes among couples precipitately married as teenagers.[6] [6: Hugh Carter and Paul C. Glick, Marriage and Divorce: A Social and Economic Study, Harvard University Press, Cambridge, Massachusetts, 1970, pp. 236-237]. The current decline in early marriages thus promises eventually to diminish the divorce rate . . . In addition, today more than two-thirds of divorced persons soon remarry.[8] [8: Carter and Glick, op. cit., p. 400], sometimes establishing more stable and loving homes for the children. This remarriage rate represents an increase of some 40 percent in the last decade.[9] [9: "Is the American Family in Danger?" loc. cit.]. Similarly, many people without children divorce several times during their lives, thus inflating the

Marriage for these men also strongly implied but didn't necessarily lead to procreation. In other words, in their minds it is the first step toward bearing children, a necessary but not in and of itself sufficient condition for the creation of a "family."

"Family," on the other hand, clearly implied the presence of children to our respondents, and it was abundantly apparent that they were anything but indifferent to the responsibilities that raising children involves. Throughout their comments to us, it was clear that these men regarded the family as the single most desirable context for childrearing. Furthermore, in contrast to the critiques of the family advanced by gender radicals, these men showed no special signs of being overly attached to the nuclear form of the institution, and in fact made frequent declarations of what we felt were sincere statements of nostalgic regret about the demise of the extended family. Declared one man, a psychologist and father of three boys who lives and practices in the Pacific Northwest:

> I do think, myself, that the decline of the family, especially for childrearing purposes, would be a loss. A good nest to emerge from is extremely important. The family is, in my mind, tremendously important . . . My wife is very oriented toward family. She grew up in a Chinese subculture—actually a kind of ghetto in a way—in Canada.

statistics. But perhaps most important is the fact that over half of all current divorces do not involve offspring.[10] [10: Carter and Glick, *op. cit.*, p. 255]. Such divorces pose little threat to the family as our key social institution.[30]

Jessie Bernard concurs:

The actions of men with respect to marriage speak far louder than words; they speak, in fact, with a deafening roar. Once men have known marriage, they can hardly live without it. Most divorced and widowed men remarry. At every age, the marriage rate for both divorced and widowed men is higher than the rate for single men. Half of all divorced white men who remarry do so within three years after divorce. Indeed it might not be far-fetched to conclude that the verbal assaults on marriage indulged in by men are a kind of compensatory reaction to their dependence on it.[31]

But she was remarkably innocent, even when I first met her, when she was 24 and had come to Chicago to go to graduate school. She had always been in a Chinese environment. She had always lived in an extended family. Every generation, all the uncles, cousins, aunts, nephews, nieces, in-laws, you name it, all of them related to each other, shared holidays together, did a lot of things together . . .

Now she is naturally still very family oriented. Her family was the most important factor in my wife's life when she was growing up. The fact that she now has her first child is very important to her.

She is simply an incredibly healthy human being, and I believe a lot of it is attributable to her family environment . . . Interestingly enough, she's also been active in the women's movement. She organized a consciousness-raising group that met for quite awhile in the early 1970's, and recently she's been instrumental in helping her sister in her fight for ordination in the Episcopal ministry. But she is adamant about the family, and I believe it's a very healthy attitude. It's not mindless: She sees the good as well as the bad about tradition, and is able to discriminate between the two. . . .

The true extended family is of course not very practicable in any kind of highly advanced industrial society, particularly one as mobile as ours, so I can't see that it's likely to make a comeback. But we do see the emergence of a kind of extended family based on other than kinship bonds—actually I guess they'd be more accurately called something else, maybe communities—even on a very small neighborhood or even single household scale—rather than families. I think we'll see more of them in the future, more cooperative efforts to share domestic burdens and tasks, particularly as inflation and energy problems become more critical.

Another man commented:

> Extended families are natural. Extended communities of people, neighbors, friends, people living along the same street, whatever it is. It's kind of unnatural for a couple to get married, and then turn the family into a little box, their own little world, one that puts them apart from everyone else. I think that's one reason people have kids, because they want to avoid the claustrophobia that can build up in a one-to-one environment. They have kids in part so they can start developing some sense of a larger community in their marriage, so they can bring the world in a little more.

• *These men felt quite emphatically that children generally need contact with both a male parent figure and a female parent figure in order to truly thrive.*
One of the men we talked to is a counselor at a larger urban high school in a solidly middle-class, well integrated neighborhood in a large city on the East Coast. His response to our questions about the issue of single-parenting was unequivocal:

> I realize the structure of the family is an extremely controversial issue right now, but all I can see are the casualties of what we used to call "broken homes" in my day. In other words, kids being raised by one parent, usually the mother in the past, but more and more often it's the father nowadays.
>
> If the kids are old enough when the parents split it's not too bad, not too hard on them. But younger

kids . . . well all I can say is that based on my experiences and the experiences of people I know well and the kids I see, it is unquestionable to me that the family, the two-parent family, is very important—maybe more important than any single other factor—for a kid's psychological well-being. As far as I'm concerned, single-parent families have just got to be, in ninety-nine percent of the cases, far tougher on both the kids *and* the parent. Aside from all the psychological pressures, there's the simple practical burden of trying to be responsible for the care of another human being, a young and more or less helpless one at that, all by yourself. The lack of privacy, the lack of a social life, the relentlessness of it, the feeling of responsibility—it's murder. And I just don't think there *are* any good ways to cope with the stress it causes. They just don't exist yet. If there ever was a job that took the energies of at least two people, and then some, it is raising kids. . . .

I have a very good friend, a carpenter. He and his wife split about a year ago, and then she died suddenly. So now he's got the child, a boy who's about six or seven now, and he's struggling to handle the whole thing. He's trying to raise the kid by himself . . . a situation that lots of women have faced for decades. He has relatives who help some, but all the same the sheer drain on his time and energy is ferocious. He's working, he's got to come home, pick the kid up from school or wherever he is that day, get his laundry, do the shopping, run the errands, throw something in the oven, and so on and so on.

It's affecting his health, and his career. He just can't concentrate, can't catch his breath, psychologically. Frankly he worries me. I try to help him out, but it's not the kind of situation where a friend

Men Respond: The Interviews

who lives halfway across town and has maybe one day a week free can really have any impact on the problem. I mean, he needs a partner. A full-time partner.

A number of men responded to our questions on this subject by referring to their own negative personal experiences of being raised by only one parent:

> I think single-parenting is very tough, especially if you're trying to raise a child of the opposite sex. Why this is, I don't know, but I feel very strongly about it . . .
> I'm an example. I love women. I love them and hate them. The hate I feel because I was left alone a lot as a kid. My father died when I was very young. I was under two, and my mother was, let's see, about twenty-six. This was in 1937. My father was forty-one, fifteen years older than my mother, which was "semi-outrageous" in those days . . . But she was a survivor, you know, she had all the right survival instincts, so when he died, she just went on with her life, and I went to live with my grandparents a lot of the time. Then when she was around, I was always having to compete with other men all the time for her attention, so naturally I developed a certain level of mistrust of women . . . Psychiatrists would say I hate women because I looked at my mother when I was young and I thought, "How come she's alive and he's dead? She must have gotten rid of him. Is she going to do that to me too? But then how come she's never around me?" . . .
> Anyway, I never talk about this stuff, and I wouldn't say I feel particularly bothered by it, or sorry for myself. But I know that being a single parent my mother was not the ideal role model for

a mother. Of course I have some of her qualities, so in a way I understand her. What could she do, with a kid . . . ?

When I was growing up, single parents were very unique. When you only have one parent when you grow up, you feel somewhat deprived and you feel like a freak, or you did in my day. It makes you intensely curious, obsessive maybe, about other kids' families. I was very aware of having only one parent, so while other kids were walking through life hardly thinking about these types of things, thinking about baseball and so on, I was into everybody's parents, into the search for a father, I suppose. As a result of all this, I have a mother figure complex the way most guys would have a mother *and* a father figure complex. I only have the mother figure to deal with, but I think it gives me a slight edge in some situations. I like strong women. I relate to women with power. I'm not threatened by them. I like it. And I have a lot of powerful women friends.

But I'm also amazed to find myself still a bachelor. I've been married once, and I always thought I would wind up married again. Now, if someone had told me in college, when I was all set to follow the same route as everyone else, that I would wind up divorced, no children, and alone when I was forty-eight, I wouldn't have believed it.

Men who emphasized the importance of the influence of both a male and a female parent on children were usually quick to add the provision that the parent couple had to be on good terms with one another and that if they were not, no child was likely to benefit from exposure to continued animosity between them. In fact, much of the enthusiasm of these men for a contemporary version of the extended family seems to stem from their appreciation of the fact that most single parents hitherto did not voluntarily choose to try to raise a child by themselves. From this point of view, the value of the extended or communal family in these men's minds was that it could still provide backup support and parent respite even if the family nucleus splits and dissolves. Generally, it might be said that these men simply felt that children benefit more from contact with a large circle of adults of both sexes than from relatively restricted exposure to the adult world.

> I think it's important for children to have a male and female parent. That's why I was saying that there should always at least be some sort of regular visitation, even in the most bitter divorce. I think courts should encourage joint custody whenever it's feasible. I think it's particularly important for a male child to have the experience of living with his father. Not having had a father, I've felt a very strong lack in that area.
> If couples do have to break up—and that will always happen—it's very important that male children have a chance to live with the father and female children have a chance to live with the mother. There has to be some sense of exposure to both experiences—maternal and paternal—for contact with the same-sex and the opposite-sex parent.
> Usually it's much too lopsided. The kid really only gets to know one parent or the other—so far it's usually been the mother. Parents have to accommodate this. Neither one should be allowed to just say, "I want the children, you can't see them except for one night a week." At that point, the parent is thinking of himself or herself, and of depriving the ex-spouse. He or she is *not* thinking of the children's welfare or well-being, and that's bad.
>
> Single parenting can work in my opinion only if the parent has access to people of the opposite sex

who can be with the kid a lot. Proximity to both sexes is important, but it doesn't have to be just one individual of either sex all the time, it can be different men, or different women, as long as a certain level of genuine interaction with the kid is reached. Usually a surrogate, a pseudo-father can be found, like a grandfather, or an uncle. I've seen kids grow up okay without a father, but they do have to have other men to hang out with.

- *These men were divided in their responses to our questions about the viability of the dual-career family.*

In our view, this subject promises to be the most complex and fateful gender-related issue of the 1980's, one that is already evoking an intense sense of interest, and some concern, in the men we interviewed. On the one hand, these men are utterly sympathetic, as we described earlier in this chapter, to the argument that women deserve equal pay for work of comparable worth to that done by male co-workers. At the same time, they are beginning to understand the momentous and far-reaching implications of the explosion in the numbers of women who are just now entering the work force.

Whereas a generation ago only about a quarter of all adult women and about one-seventh of all wives worked, today, according to the Department of Labor, approximately three-fifths of all American families contain at least two wage earners. Almost sixty percent of all American wives work, and that figure is not likely to decline within the foreseeable future. However, again according to the Department of Labor, women employed full-time earn only about 60 cents for every dollar earned by men. Female college graduates' starting salaries average $7000 *less* than the starting salary of the average male college graduate.

As far as the men we spoke to are concerned, there simply is no legitimate defense for this kind of gross salary inequity. But it should also be noted that there are some recent signs that this discriminatory disparity is beginning to change, at least in certain areas. *Time* magazine reports in its issue of March 17, 1980, that an American Chemical Society study found that "women graduates in chemistry now get better salary offers than their male classmates. In 1979 the median starting salary of women with a bachelor's degree in chemistry was $15,600, compared with $15,000 for men. For women who specialized in chemical engineering, the median starting salary was $20,000 vs. $19,800 for men."[32] *Time* quotes an American Chemical Society spokesman as saying "a lot of employers are beginning to wake up to the fact that they have discriminated against women in the past."

We think most men are also quite willing to share more equally in early parenting, childrearing, and other domestic maintenance chores. That equality means a larger male role in the household as well as a larger female role in the workplace is an argument that was readily sanctioned by the men we spoke to. We did have the opportunity to talk to two couples who were managing to make dual-career households work very well.

John and Terry Trumbull live in the heart of the midwest, Des Moines, Iowa. He is a successful real estate broker, she is an attorney, practicing in partnership with her husband's brother Richard. Both in their late thirties, John and Terry have two children, a son, Daniel, aged eleven, and a daughter, Linda, aged eight.

John and Terry believe that their marriage is a good example of how a dual-career family can work even with children. They have thought a great deal about their mutual accommodation and how the division of labor works in their marriage.

> John: I'd been married once before, in my early twenties, and it hadn't worked out, of course, so I was a shade more reluctant than Terry was at first to try it again. She handled my hesitation about it very well. She didn't seem to feel any great, special urgency about it and completely hung loose the whole time. As a matter of fact, that was a great

strategy. It just made her seem even more attractive to me, since I had really been pushed into marrying by the previous woman, who was already picking out the silverware patterns when we'd only known each other a few weeks. That turned me off completely, but I was too young and too intimidated by women in general back then to say anything about it.

I also remember feeling a little concerned because Terry seemed like such an accomplished woman already, such an intellectual. Maybe I was a little overawed by the fact that she was in law school, but I can remember one thing I really wanted to straighten out before we got married was whether or not she was planning to pursue a really heavily career-oriented lifestyle . . . the workaholic kind of thing. That was one very definite concern I had. I knew she wanted her career, and that was actually very attractive to me, but I didn't want it to exclude all the other things I wanted—family, leisure, just having time to enjoy life together—all that. I knew how those things could get squeezed out of anyone's life very quickly from my own stint as a workaholic, and I didn't want to have it happen again in my family life.

All she said when I asked her about it was that she thought she was as interested as I was in having a family too, not just her career, that she definitely knew she wanted the experience of being a mother, and that she knew she would regret it if she missed it, or didn't do it right.

Terry is definitely the most important thing in my life, she and the kids. For them to be happy is very important to me, and has been all throughout our relationship. We don't seem to get into some of the kinds of tangles that other people do, but I'm not sure why. I suspect it's because we're so normal, and normalcy just doesn't tend to have as much gossip value as those situations where people are having trouble in their marriages.

You know how it is, people tend to fixate on the negative: John Jones has an affair one night in some little suburban village and pretty soon that gets blown all the hell out of proportion, and pretty soon everyone is hysterical about what is happening to the nuclear family and will it survive and all that. When things are sound and sane in relationships, it's somewhat too ordinary for people who are addicted to the sensationalizing that we get exposed to so much in this culture. . . .

Of course, having children does change your life profoundly. Formerly it was just the two of us, Terry and me, for each other, sharing all the interesting things this community has to offer—plays, ballet, music, football—and most of all, our feelings about each other and about our work. Then suddenly, it became the two of us for Danny and Lin. We had less time for each other, less time to share our personal feelings with each other, less time to just talk about what we did during the day, about what had happened to us and so on.

And that means you get just a bit isolated from each other when you have kids, because it's so much harder to stay current, to stay in touch with what's happening in your spouse's life. But the gap isn't so wide when you divide the labor of making a living and of raising the kids more or less evenly between you. It's not so much like you live in two different worlds—one of which is the "big picture" realm of work, and the other is the minutiae of getting kids to school and answering their questions and just generally keeping track of what's going on with them. So I think two-career families have that one big built-in advantage: there's no way for things to get so completely polarized in terms of functions that the man can't talk to the woman and vice versa.

On the other hand, it's important to maintain a little flexibility. You can't expect to divide every task neatly down the middle and give half to the woman and half to the man. It just never works out that way. For example, I've always taken the garbage out, all the time we've been together, and Terry has cleaned the stove. I've always washed the windows and she's always washed the car, or had it washed. Somehow, for us, those are a couple of the things that just happened naturally, those particular divisions.

Same with the kids. For some reason I've tended to be the one, most of the time, who takes them out to get new clothes and haircuts and to the doctor for minor checkups, and Terry's usually been the one who makes time in her schedule to go to the parent-teacher meetings at school and to check out their extracurricular activities. It's not a hard and fast division—sometimes we switch roles in those areas—but there are these natural apportionments that show up in making your life together, and I think they should be taken advantage of, not resisted. It shouldn't be that every time she makes a meat loaf then I owe her one meat loaf. That gets awfully tense in a hurry. As long as both partners feel that they're getting as much as they're giving, in a general sort of way, then I don't think it helps to worry too much about issues like, Is one person getting more free time than the other, or Are the jobs I have to do more demanding than the ones she has to do?

Another thing about having kids, is that you are

suddenly busier than you ever were before, but you're also somewhat lonelier than ever before, especially in a two-career family, because there just is less time for everyone to be together. I mean, when Daddy's got the kids to take them out somewhere, most of the time Mommy has to go to the office. She can't just tag along and enjoy the trip too. So you have to have a good strong relationship, a good understanding and sense of commitment between you *before* the kids come along, so you know that you can be somewhat cut off from each other when they do arrive, and that you can depend on the other person to do their share of the work, and that there's no subterranean resentment brewing about being somewhat isolated and lonely all of a sudden. And it's also good to try very specifically to set aside certain times when the whole family is together, once a week, or every other week, for awhile.

At first we had occasional conflicts with the kids about what is parents' time to be together, what is parents' time to be with the kids. They are very demanding. And in a way, they should be. You want to love them unconditionally while they're little so that they get over it, get weaned from needing it quite so much, so they can grow up to be self-sufficient adults.

But there are times when you also have to deny them, to say, "No, now it's our time to be with each other for awhile, so leave us alone for a few minutes." Of course, it gets much better when they get old enough to go to school, start making their own friends, get involved with sports and all that. Then they start to grow away from you and that makes you a little sad at first, when you first start to feel it happening, start to feel the great big bad old world slowly drawing them away. But then even at that stage there are compensations, because you notice that you begin to draw closer to your mate again, that you can finally begin to turn toward each other again in a way that's even richer in some ways, friendlier in some ways, than it was before the kids came along.

But when they're little there's always a little competition for your time. They don't really want you to talk to each other, to exclude them, they want you to talk to them. But even that's basically a positive and loving thing.

Another thing is income. I had always thought of myself as a realist, economically speaking, and the thought of having two incomes in a family, as long as you could shelter it from the tax bite somehow, seemed like a big plus to me. No two ways about it. There would be more expenses for childcare, eating out, domestic help now and then, but on balance you'd come out ahead.

Well, I still think that's true. But what I didn't really anticipate, since I like to think of myself as being so level-headed and objective, psychologically, was that as Terry's income began to creep up toward mine, and then keep right on going past it, especially during those years like 1974 and in there, when money was tight and business was so bad, it really kind of rattled me to think that she was making more money than I was.

We actually had some squabbles about it, all provoked by the most ridiculous kinds of things, things like balancing the checkbook. I kind of began to feel like even though we were both doing well in terms of bringing money into the family, I was the only one who was really having to work to keep track of where it was going. I was the one paying all the bills, balancing the checkbook, projecting the cash flow, all that. As her income began to exceed mine, it became more and more of a burden to me. I really began to feel put out about having to keep track of it all, like I wasn't getting any real cooperation from her, like she thought all she had to do was make it, not worry about how we spent it. I started to accuse her of spending too much, just when she was making more than either one of us had ever before in our entire lives.

Terry: That really astonished me. Here I was, finally making some grand theft bread, and John was turning into a miser right before my very eyes. I just couldn't understand it, it was so contrary. Why did he want to have me suddenly become so obsessed with where it was going, now that I was finally really bringing it in? I thought he was trying to make me feel guilty, like I was some kind of spendthrift, and that just made me angry.

John: Yeah, eventually I realized that I was just feeling nervous and resentful because she was able to afford to be so relaxed about it. It was like some kind of reproach to me, as though she was saying, "Oh, you worry about where it goes, since I'm the one who brings it in." It just felt really irritating to me, like she was constantly reminding me, through her indifference to money, that she was the one who was making it. I took it personally.

I still feel uncomfortable about admitting it, but it made me feel damned insecure. I don't think most men are prepared for that yet, not most men of my age and background, but it's not all that hard to cope with. Terry and I talked about it and pretty much resolved it, but I still get twinges of guilt, or inferiority, or competitiveness, or whatever it is.

Actually, now that I'm talking about it I can

think of some men I know who would have a much harder time with it than me, men who have a hard time acknowledging any achievements their wives make, even if it's something as trivial as winning a tennis tournament. Those guys are really gonna have it tough when their wives start to bring in an income or get promoted up to high-powered jobs with titles and salaries that match theirs. I think that's still going to be a tough problem for some men. Not all, but some for sure.

In terms of logistics, I guess all I can think of is that you need clearcut routines, clear mutual agreements about who's supposed to handle which kinds of tasks and responsibilities. Then you need good follow-through. You need to know that each person is going to keep his or her end of the bargain. It's like anything else, any other kind of teamwork. If she says that she's going to get the car filled up for me, then she'd better do it so I don't have to fit time into my schedule to make up for her slips. And it works the same way in reverse. If I say I'll check the oil in the car, then I'd sure as hell better do it, because she doesn't have time in her busy life to get stranded on the highway, any more than I do.

Terry: Aside from assigned tasks, especially where the kids are concerned, since they're so unpredictable in many ways, we've always followed a policy of just doing whatever needs to be done. Whoever can handle it does it. That's where you need a sense of flexibility to complement the cut-and-dried assignments, cause kids don't always follow your programs and you can't stand on ceremony when they suddenly need something. You have to be able to handle situations based on what's necessary, as well as on set patterns. Whatever is necessary, do it. It's not so hard. In fact it's natural if you care about your husband and your family. The result is the main thing, so you just concentrate on that. If there's a disaster, no amount of trying to fix blame or equal it out after the fact is going to change or salvage anything then.

John: Flexibility is important too because you both have long days, you get home, you're tired, and you still need to get dinner and do whatever you need to do. And sometimes your plans get upset. She has to work late, or go back to the office, or I've got to get back to a client in half an hour, whatever. So you learn to improvise. Again, it's teamwork. Those things happen. It's part of the ballgame. You get disappointments. You have to learn to expect that when you're both busy people and you have kids. Roll with it, adapt, and enjoy it as much as possible. Set up the basis of as many pre-assigned kinds of things as possible, then let the rest happen as it seems best at the time. It happens. I'll come home, all ready to go out, or something, and she'll remind me that she has a PTA meeting to get to. Things like that.

I'm just glad that neither one of us has to travel much in our jobs, because that would really put a bind on the one left at home. When that kind of thing has happened in the past, we've just hired someone we can rely on to help take care of the kids. I think that's the only way you can handle it, unless you're lucky enough to have an in-law handy who can help out.

The whole thing takes a lot of work, but if you've got *commitment* and *patience*, lots and lots of patience, it's workable, and infinitely worthwhile.

Clearly, one of the critical variables that can make or break the two-paycheck household is money. If there is sufficient income, the couple's lifestyle can be maintained and domestic assistance can be procured as necessary. These men, we discovered, were not particularly receptive to the alternative of "voluntary simplicity," that is, the choice of reducing material needs rather than increasing income. Instead, they wanted the sense of independence and freedom that comes with material affluence. They didn't particularly care which partner was primarily responsible for earning the income to make such a lifestyle feasible. They did believe that, since money is the single most important facilitating factor in making lifestyle options possible, the wishes of whoever was earning the most money should in certain respects be deferred to.

> But the point is that in an adult-to-adult relationship, whether it is the man or the woman who is making more money, well I think one of the practicalities that both partners in the relationship have to address is the issue of who is contributing the most, *materially*, to supporting their lifestyle. Whoever is making the most money, whoever is contributing the most to *paying* the way, to maintaining the lifestyle, then I think both partners should basically defer to her or him. Doesn't matter whether it's the man or the woman, in fact I can't wait to marry a woman who makes a half-million dollars a year so I can find out how it works going the other way. But it should be equal, in my view. If she's supporting me, then I defer to her.

In the case of complete role exchange that we encountered, where a man had left his career to become a househusband while his wife had assumed total responsibility for the role of breadwinner in the family, we found that this masculine deference to economic clout had often had significant repercussions in the couple's patterns of sexual interaction.

> The person that holds the economic pursestrings really wields a lot of power. You know, I defer to

my wife, not in a humiliating way, but in a natural way. I think it's right. I worked, I had a career, I know what the pressures are like. So now, if we make plans to go out, to a movie or something, and she comes home like I used to and says, "I just want to get something to eat, or go for a walk, I'm too tired for the movie," I go along with it. I say, "Oh fine."

It's affected our sexual roles. In a traditional marriage, if a woman felt romantic, she could wait until the man came home and then seduce him. The candle-lit dinner, and all that. There were ways to unlock the responses she wanted in him. By the same token, the man might sort of fluff up his feathers, put on a little cologne, and strut his stuff. But when you reverse the roles, and she's the one who's coming home and saying, "Whew, am I tired! I've got this splitting headache," or "I've really got too much work to do tonight honey, so you go on to bed without me," you don't have any choice but to give way to it. I mean it's pretty silly to think that you're going to start asserting yourself along like the old lines: "Baby, wait until you get home tonight." My wife is a powerful executive, not a "baby."

That's a tricky situation, one that we've talked about a lot, one that we're still dealing with, and one that I don't have any simple solutions for. That's the major question that reversal of roles has raised for me.

One man cautioned that even a two-paycheck income could be a deceptive advantage:

> We were making a lot of money when we both worked, but we were burning a lot of money up doing it too. At one point during the five-year interval when we both worked we had four cars, for

some reason. We owned two properties, but taxes were killing us. We ate out a lot because we'd both get home after work and there would be two hungry kids staring at us and nothing in the refrigerator because no one had time to go shopping. Financially, we didn't find that the reward was there. We looked good on paper, and we had a lot of cash coming in, but we had one hell of a cash hemorrhage too.

We do not feel that this emphasis on income was in any way a conscious or unconscious sexist subterfuge on the part of these men, a vehicle designed to allow them to reassert a sense of masculine primacy in the middle of an era of confusing role flux. As we describe below, the "househusband" in our sample, who had experienced total reversal of roles, expressed precisely the same belief in a bedrock deference to the first priority of the couple: making a living.

These men also acknowledged that the issue of income can put most women in a difficult, chicken-and-egg type double bind: Male emphasis on the relative wage-earning potential of each partner as the foremost consideration in appraising work vs. domestic roles, when combined with the discriminatory reality that women generally still do not earn as much as men do, seems to put these men in the position of endorsing the perpetuation of *de facto* sexism in the marketplace. Perhaps so. We believe the response of most of these men to this charge would be oblique. They would instead stress the importance of allowing for sufficient time to effect the economic readjustments generally occasioned by a shift of roles and to do so without overlooking the fundamental, central importance of the wage-earning function in any relationship, even if at present it is necessarily conducted in an occupational environment that is undeniably sexist.

You know what's really crazy about this thing, the women's movement, is that in spite of the fact that women are totally right, I mean that there's no way you can fault their arguments on the level of justice, equal pay for equal work, that kind of thing, this is economically absolutely the wrong time for this kind of mass value shift to be happening. Inflation is making the two-paycheck family necessary at exactly the same time as unemployment is climbing, there're fewer jobs, and there's a lot more competition for those that are opening up. Now women are flooding into the labor force. I personally believe we're going to see more job-sharing in the future, with a man and woman sharing a job, so they can both work and both take care of the home and kids. But I don't think that's going to really solve *all* the problems we're going to encounter in this area.

A second reservation about dual-career households voiced by these men had to do with the quality of time a couple spends together and with their view that any relationship needs to provide some respite and rejuvenation to whichever partner(s) is (are) experiencing the stress of competing in the marketplace. Citing the inescapable pressures involved in any demanding career, these men pointed to the danger of mutual burnout, even in circumstances where there was adequate income to purchase sufficient domestic assistance to keep the household clean and orderly.

For a while we were both very busy and our careers were moving along nicely, but it was draining us, psychologically. We had drawn up clearcut goals before we moved here, like having a nice home, entertaining, having children, a myriad of other things that we both wanted. So we came out here, and our original plan was to live in a co-op but that became impossible because of our dog, so we bought a house in the suburbs.

We had an agreement: Pat would cook, I would clean. It doesn't bother me in the least to vacuum a rug or do the dishes, whatever. But as we got caught up in the pressures of our jobs, things began to come unglued. Pat was working for a cosmetics firm, as a regional sales representative, and it required her to do a lot of traveling, especially on weekends, to a lot of the big shopping centers around here, and sometimes she would be away overnight, or even all weekend, which was my time off.

Well, I didn't much like being home alone, sticking frozen food in the microwave, and waiting for her to call, so I began to work on the weekends too. Pretty soon we were both so strung out that we would go out and do our thing workwise and get so exhausted by it that by the time we got home there wasn't any energy left over. And as a result the house just become a dropoff place to dump the dirty laundry, get a little sleep, clean up, put on fresh clothes, and take off again. It was a good thing we didn't have kids. We just couldn't have handled it.

Anyway, as a result of this, the whole relationship deteriorated into something that, honestly, was less than you would have going with just a roommate. We had no time together at all, certainly no quality time, no relaxed time together. It was just ships passing in the night, and all that. The house was just a convenience. If we saw each other, fine. If we didn't, no big deal. All the plans we had never materialized, and I finally said, "Well if this is the way it's going to be, I don't want it." So I filed for divorce last June.

The final significant reservation these men expressed about the two-career household sounds the theme of our earlier discussion in this chapter of the effect on children of growing up with only very limited supervision from parents who are preoccupied by their careers. For many busy professional couples, successful child-rearing depends upon obtaining intelligent, talented, resourceful housekeepers. Said a female child psychologist practicing in New York:

> I see, very commonly, two-career families in which the kid is very fucked up. Maybe they're both doctors, or attorneys, or something else, but they've both got demanding careers that neither one wants to give up, so the upshot is that no one is on top of what's happening with the kid. The kids are being taken care of by a succession of temporaries who often have their own kids at home to think about and they're just not going to be that involved in this strange kid's well-being.
>
> For example, I had a patient whose daughter went to a very exclusive private school and was the only kid in the class who wasn't able to read on the first day. Everybody else, all the other kids, had already been taught by their parents how to read. It was like a fad. Everyone was doing it. It was what was *in* that year. But this kid, her parents were so absorbed by their careers, they weren't keeping track of what was happening in other families. They weren't going down to the park to talk to the other mothers. They weren't part of the informal informational network that naturally springs up around parents of relatively young children.
>
> My husband and I *know* that we have to keep track of our kids because things happen suddenly in kids' lives. They erupt. You have to be part of the community, the network that develops around these things. It's incredibly important. One or the other of us, my husband or I, makes it a point to

talk to the teachers when we drop the kids off at school on the way to work, and the other mothers. But a lot of the other parents don't, and that's what happened to this little girl who came to see me. You can't just do it mechanically, drop the kids off and go to work. You do that, and they get the worst teachers, they get with the worst other kids, they don't know who's crazy and who isn't, all that. You have to know the situation, so that if there's a problem, you can deal with it effectively.

Anyway so this kid couldn't read and it made her self-conscious, of course. She felt left out and stupid so she refused to go to school, or she would go and then after her folks had dropped her off, she'd hop in a cab and go home. She presented as a school phobic. But it was just that her parents were so involved in their careers that they—they were perfectly adequate parents—but they left a lot up to the maid, and it had never crossed their minds to try to teach their daughter to read *before* she went to school for the first time. They just dealt with it all literal-mindedly, and, as it turned out, they caused their kid a lot of unnecessary pain.

Similarly, it was the negative effect on his youngest son that made Gerald Rissler, owner of a San Francisco restaurant, first consider selling his business and letting his wife become the sole breadwinner in their family while he stayed home and transformed himself into a househusband:

My wife Elaine and I had been married for, oh, about twenty-three years when we made this decision. We were both working at the time—she's now a vice-president in a bank that's headquartered here—and it's now been three years, and I feel it's working out fine. The idea originally came up because our youngest son—we have three boys, who are now fifteen, eighteen, and twenty-one—was having a lot of trouble at school and getting into drugs and we got worried about him. So we started talking about it, questioning the tendency to just do what everybody else was doing, the rat race, no time at home, all that, and we carefully planned it for a good year or so before I put the business up for sale.

I probably couldn't have even considered it if I had had serious qualms about women in the marketplace, if I felt very threatened by the thought of my wife being out there all day with a bunch of men. Still I did have to do a certain amount of work on myself. I had to go through some steps to first realize how chauvinistic I was, and maybe still am, and then try to come to terms with this shift in our roles, mine especially.

But we did it, and I sold the business, and then suddenly I was home all day, and she was becoming more and more involved with her career, having to stay at work late, or calling me and telling me she wouldn't be home for lunch, and all her conversations about her co-workers were about other men, since that's who she works with, mostly. Banking is still primarily dominated by men. Those kinds of things still stung a little bit, I found, much to my chagrin.

But I think I've come to grips with it, and now I have no real problem with it, even when Elaine has to be out of town for a few days. She went to Washington last year to testify at some hearing, and I didn't really mind, although I missed her. Now she's about to go to New York. It's just become a matter of that's the way it is.

It definitely became easier to run this household and relate to one another as a family during that first year that I was home. And that's why I'm dubious about the possibility of most two-career families managing to make it work. It was only because we had energies freed up that we had been using for our careers that we pulled ourselves back together as a family, or even as a couple. We finally had some energy left for each other. Most two-career homes are overstressed. I know ours was.

It's been my observation that even when there are no children in the relationship, there is still a lot of stress in the relationships among our friends who are both working. Most of them eventually split up. It's sad, but that's the truth. We are now left with mostly single friends. I don't know whether we have twice as many or half as many now. But I do know there are fewer and fewer couples. The marketplace of the 1970's, and of the 1980's too I'm sure, is just too demanding for couples to make it, by and large, unless they are unusual, extraordinary people.

There's also a current tendency to shy away from traditional values, a certain attitude of just wanting to dump it all, toss it all out, start all over from fresh. I think that contributes to these couples not staying together. I also think that will change. I think it will have to. . . .

Now that I am a full-fledged househusband, I am finding that the complaint of women in the past that the role of homemaker is an undcrappreciated one is certainly true. It doesn't matter who is filling that role, a man or a woman, people don't know how to react to it, and they definitely aren't very interested in it. In our personal situation, with Elaine and I, since we both know both sides of the coin, since we've both had demanding jobs and have both been homemakers, she has a great appreciation for what I have to do to keep the household intact, and I have a great appreciation and sympathy for what she has to do to make it in the marketplace.

But when I walk out the door, I often feel suddenly like I've become invisible, insignificant. People out there—men or women—don't really want to talk about me being a househusband. Women don't really believe that's what I am. Men feel threatened. There's a certain kind of curiosity, but damned little honesty.

Men tend to immediately overcompensate by demonstrating how important they are. The other night I went to drop by some friends who are still in the restaurant business, people I used to work with. I walked into the gentleman's office and said, "How are you?" He looked up and said, "Our gross is up." I thought, Uh, oh, I shouldn't have bothered to stop by—might as well turn around and leave again. There wasn't a person there, there was a role. That happens in business, but I find it's hard to bridge the gap and that most men aren't really interested in trying.

Occasionally these days when we go out in public, to a party or whatever, I just say I'm a writer, or a consultant. I don't like to lie, neither does my wife, but it's easier, most people aren't going to know how to react if I say, "I'm a househusband."

I've noticed definite changes in myself in these three years. I'm becoming more relaxed. More Type B, less Type A. If I were to describe myself to you as I was a decade ago, you wouldn't believe the contrast. Then I was stubborn, bullheaded, aggressive, bad-tempered. I had to be, just to keep the business in the black. There were times when I felt like I was so mad I could eat the plaster right off the wall. Now I don't get so overworked about things. I work hard, but I don't take myself so seriously. I feel more settled, more relaxed, more calmed down. I like it. . . .

I still have to work on developing better communication with my kids. That's an area I'm still working on. You know, it's one of the effects of playing that breadwinner role and being out of the house so much. When they were little, before Elaine went back to work, she was the one who dressed them to go to school and took care of their scrapes and bruises and handled that kind of thing. That establishes pretty deep bonds that still tend to dictate their behavior. For example, I know that even now when they have a problem they still go talk to her about it. They just feel more comfortable with her. But that is changing, slowly. Generally, I think we all communicate better in this household since I made this role shift. . . .

The most important thing about the way we have the roles arranged now is that there is a totally clear division of labor. We know exactly who has to do what. I take care of everything in the house. I pay all the bills. We don't have to struggle to improvise each time something causes us to change our plans. People who both work may know that they are overstressed, but they don't usually have time to stop and evaluate the real costs of it all. They don't figure out how the lack of clear assignments of responsibilities is really costing them a lot of time and energy.

We have friends, even couples—a few of them—with no children, who go around and around about how often he is supposed to clean the bathroom and how often she is supposed to fix supper. It becomes a major hassle in their lives. It's silly. People who come home tired from work shouldn't have to renegotiate every little detail of their domestic arrangement, and that's where I think a lot of two-career families get tripped up. . . .

• *None of these men were in any way worried about the possibility that their children—boys or girls—would suffer from sex-role stereotyping in the future.*

The men we interviewed were by and large unconcerned about the possible effect of sex-role stereotyping on their children. They almost unanimously expressed unqualified confidence in the ability of their offspring to remain healthy, clearsighted, and unaffected in negative ways by the gender turbulence of the last two decades.

> I think the kids are basically fine. This whole uproar about equality is only a very minor adjustment for them. Sure it trickles down to their level, and it will change their lives in many ways, but it won't be anything dramatic for them. I mean, I think now, at fifteen, Sean is much more accepting of the fact that women can be leaders, do the same kinds of jobs that men can, stuff like that. But I remember as a real little kid, one time his sister said she wanted to be a policeman and he said something like, "Women can't be policemen." That's what is changing, and in no small part due to deliberate efforts on the part of me and Marlene. For instance, I remember we were driving alone one day in the car and we overheard Brenda talking to one of her little chums in the back seat about "I should grow up and marry a doctor or a lawyer," and I said, "Why don't you grow up to *be* a doctor or a lawyer?"
>
> Neither my wife nor I regard the issue of raising a masculine child during a time of changing role models as posing any kind of real problem. My

wife's experiences as a child were so good under the traditional family situation—you know, where boys are boys and girls are girls—that there just doesn't seem to be any kind of basic problem about it to her. And this is, as you know, a woman who has created a demanding career for herself as a pediatrician and who seems to me to fully embody the best that the idea of a "liberated" woman has to offer . . . On the other hand, we don't really *emphasize* masculinity with Christopher. For example, he enjoys sitting at the kitchen counter and helping Sarah bake a cake or make biscuits for breakfast or something like that. He brings them in to me and says, "Look what Mommy and I made for you." He gets both experiences, because we don't insist on that rigid distinction between "that's what boys do" and "this is what girls do."

****

We have two children, one's a girl, six, and the other's a boy, eight. Neither feels confined by their identities of being a girl or a boy. Frances, our little girl, she's not concerned about being able to do what the boys do. In fact, she definitely doesn't want to do what the boys do sometimes. There are things the boys do that she doesn't want to do. Sometimes I notice that although Ronnie, our son, likes to go with me to work, to the yard, Frances tends to feel that it's boring. I get to a point now where I say to her, "Do you want to go to the yard with me?" and I kind of secretly hope she's going to say no, because I know that if she comes along she's going to be down there half the day bitching, complaining, moaning and groaning about it—she's going to be a pain in the ass. But at the same time, I always make a point of making the offer to her, though these days she'll usually come up with something else she wants to do more. She'll say, "No, I'll stay here and do this or do that." . . .

They both like to build things. See that car [pointing to a simple wooden model of an automobile]? I have a box in my shop in the garage that's full of old scraps, odds and ends that I pick up at the yard. And they both like to go down there and get the glue and the hammer and the nails and make things. She's down there as much as Ronnie is. She does as much of it as he does. . . .

We feel that we're very sensitive to the influences that kids pick up outside the home, especially in school, and so far we can't see that they're being socialized in any kind of stereotypical way. They are fortunate because they go to a very good school, where the emphasis is on confidence, not on becoming just like everyone else, or on conforming to a preestablished model of behavior, or anything like that. Francie says the same thing Ronnie does, "I can be anything I want." And we tell them the same thing. . . .

On the other hand, there's no question in my mind that she does like to do things that we think of as traditionally girlish. There's an interesting situation that developed here just recently with her uncle, who adores her, and in fact makes Ronnie feel a little left out sometimes, which kind of bothered us for a while. He lives and breathes flyfishing and loves to take her out with him when he goes out for the day. But now these last few times that they were over, he's started taking Ronnie instead because he'd ask Francie if she wanted to go and she sure could have. But she chose to stay home with Aunt Lynn and bake a cake. They came home from fishing last weekend and she told them what a good time she and Lynn had had when the boys were gone. We know we're not doing it, that we're not creating situations that subtly encourage her to do one thing or the other.

****

I have two children, a boy and a girl. My son is still quite young, thirteen, but my daughter is now twenty-three, and I can't see that her attitude toward herself, her role, or toward men is in any way constrained or limited by any kind of preconceived attitudes. I think she really knows what she wants and is willing to dedicate herself to looking for it, and I think her values are heartfelt and work for her. Most important, though, is that she judges things on an individual basis, she has the maturity to understand that you can only generalize so far, and she's not especially gullible, not especially taken in by the kind of heavily sensationalized images we all get bombarded by these days.

Take sex. Her sexual values, which are entirely her own, could in some ways be described as quite traditional. She has a very healthy attitude toward men. She instinctively felt that she didn't want a sexual experience until it was with someone she would care for. And it wasn't because either my wife or I indoctrinated her, it was just the way she felt. Then when she was twenty, she had a boyfriend, someone I knew, a very gentle, thoughtful man, and she told us when they started sleeping together. It wasn't impulsive, or because others were doing it. She's always been much more her own person than that—sensitive and intelligent and well thought out, deliberate, I guess you could say.

So I just feel that, as far as I can tell, based on

my own experiences within my own family, with my own daughter, there's no likelihood of any kind of stereotype having all that powerful an effect on the attitudes and behavior of future generations. I think we're getting away from that, thanks to the women's movement, but I think the real value of the movement, the real meaning of liberation, is that our kids know they have the freedom to make up their own minds, as individuals, to do what's right for them, and not to follow *any* kind of model or pre-programmed pattern, if it isn't what they really want. Whatever liberation and independence there's been on my daughter's part, it's been of a kind that's made her a more enlightened and effective individual, as far as I can see.

****

Naturally my daughter's attitudes about her future are in a period of constant change, but then that's nothing extraordinary—all of our attitudes change all the time, no matter how old we are. None of us sees things the same as he or she did ten years ago. But since she's only seventeen, it's hard to tell how much of that is due to the women's movement and how much isn't. I'd be inclined to say it's more likely just the normal changes anyone at that age experiences. I don't think Melanie—my daughter—is significantly different in her attitudes than, say, my own sister Amanda—who would be sixty-three if she were still alive—was at her age, at Melanie's stage of development.

She is highly interested in the natural sciences, and is therefore attracted to fields that have been heavily male-dominated, in their professional applications anyway. She loves being outdoors, putting on her high-top boots, going out and looking under rocks, catching bugs with her net, and all those other things. She just thinks all that's super, so there you are.

And yet, in so many other ways she's very, very feminine in an entirely traditional way. I'm sure when the right young man comes along and pops the question, she'll say yes. So there you are again.

****

My daughter is kind of an exceptional child—she's almost twenty-one now—in that she attended all-girl, parochial schools until she went to college. So until she was eighteen or so, she only competed with other women, which is unusual in this day and age. Personally, I think it was quite good for her. Her identity as a person was well-formed before she had to confront the whole issue of gender identity in a male-dominated culture.

And Carolyn definitely has a very strong sense of her own identity. The whole problem of feeling that she is being repressed by a stereotyped female role is really not an issue with her. She's quite conscious of herself as a woman, as an attractive female, and she works to stay attractive, but she's also comfortable with herself as a person, and has no problem dealing with men forthrightly as friends, as human beings who just happen to be male. I don't sense that there's any confusion in her between her personality and her powers of sexual attraction. She seems to me to be entirely comfortable about the whole issue, not at all resentful or depressed because she's a woman—quite the opposite.

• *Though the termination of a relationship into which one has poured heartfelt affection and energy is, of course, as painful* for women as men, both sexes were inclined to agree in these interviews that the initiation of the termination by the woman often poses special problems for the man.

Our conventional expectation is that it has usually been the man who becomes restless and claustrophobic in a relationship and walks out, leaving the woman to cope with her feelings of abandonment and rejection. Traditionally, he is the villain, she the victim. He was expected to feel guilty, she was supposed to feel hurt, helpless, and frightened at being on her own.

Now the tables are turned. Now it is, as often as not, the woman who feels the overwhelming need to break out and does so, and it is the man who is forced to suffer the consequences. But there is an important difference. Though the roles are reversed, the emotions of each partner do not always follow suit. She may feel a measure of remorse, but it is often quickly dispelled by her exhilaration at finally being on her own. He, on the other hand, is likely to find that playing the unaccustomed role of reactive victim rather than precipitating villain only magnifies his sense of guilt.

The traditional assignment of responsibility for the couple's material well-being to the man makes him susceptible to feeling like a failure when separation means that his partner is on her own. If he is continuing to help provide for her in some way financially, as was almost invariably the case with the men we interviewed, he is likely to experience obsessive misgivings about her ability to prosper without him, and to suffer from the irrational conviction that his sudden estrangement from her was in some way due to his shortcomings as a provider. Furthermore, men are also in general still much more likely to be unpleasantly surprised by the intensity of the grief and anger that they are likely to feel in these circumstances, and much less well-equipped to cope with them.

> I just went crazy at that point. I felt a combination of panic, anger, remorse, self-blame, total claustrophobia, like the world was coming to an end. I couldn't sleep, work, drive my car, you name it. I was a mess.

As Dorothy Dinnerstein has persuasively argued, men may experience profound anxiety at separation from a woman because of their primal association of physical and psychological reassurance with an infuriatingly uncontrollable female source, the mother. Women, according to Dinnerstein, are less vulnerable to the same degree of separation anxiety because they can literally embody the nurturing function that they too encountered as helpless infants. They are less estranged from that nurturing function than men and thus less threatened by its disappearance.[33]

To simplify Dinnerstein's argument, because an infant's first experience with humans is primarily with the mother the infant grows up associating femaleness with a primitive source of love, comfort, and physical nourishment. At the same time, when that love and comfort is temporarily but arbitrarily withdrawn, as it often is in any infant's life, terrifying deprivation is experienced.

In other words, an infant learns (a) that its surroundings, the source of all physical and emotional good, are unpredictable and are not under its control, and (b) that this autonomy is associated with femaleness, with women, with a mother.

Dinnerstein then argues that this powerful early experience of great but unreliable pleasure leads to the development of a strong ambivalence toward women on the part of "mother-raised," i.e., virtually *all*, men and women.

Women, she asserts, can to a certain extent internalize the loved/feared mother as they grow older, become sexually mature, and bear and raise their own children. Men, however, are more or less permanently estranged from the female source of life that they grew up needing, longing for, and fearing being deprived of because of its autonomy. Thus, Dinnerstein concludes, the special terror of men suddenly deprived of an intense relationship with a woman is a form of re-experiencing the profound helplessness of infancy, one that men are less well-equipped to transcend as adults than women are.

> The child's bodily tie to the mother, then, is the vehicle through which the most fundamental feel-

ings of a highly complex creature are formed and expressed. At her breast, it is not just a small furnace being stoked: It is a human being discovering its first great joy, handling its first meeting with a separate creature enormously more powerful than itself, living out its first awareness of wanting something for which it must depend on someone else, someone who is imperfectly benevolent and imperfectly reliable because she is (although the infant, of course, has no way of knowing that she is) also a human being. This tie is the prototype of the tie to life. The pain in it, and the fear of being cut off from it, are prototypes of the pain of life and the fear of death.[34]

Dinnerstein's theory is an invaluable contribution to the gender debate. It provides an extremely useful conceptual starting point for men and women to re-evaluate their relationship to the traditional gender roles that most of us have internalized somewhat uncritically. Certainly Dinnerstein's interpretation makes the special vulnerability of men to sex-role reversal stress much more intelligible in many ways, and provides a basis for understanding the remarkable intensity of the shock of some men when faced with a woman's unilateral decision to end their relationship.

Typically, the men we interviewed described a pattern of disengagement from relationships. First, men pass through an acute stage of brief but intense, even agonizing despair and sorrow that lasted only a few days in most instances. The second stage consisted of a period of protracted regret and mourning, low-grade depression, and intermittent bouts of sharp nostalgia for the loss of intimate companionship. Occasionally, long after it is clear to everyone else, including his ex-partner, that the relationship is irrevocably over, a deserted male will continue to entertain unrealistic hopes for a reconciliation. This latter stage can sometimes last for years.

When Connie told me she was going to marry

this guy Paul it was perhaps the most devastating piece of news I have ever had in my life. Because at the time I thought I was—and I believe I was—in love with her. I had suspected something was happening with her, but I was hoping it wasn't true. I mean I had a strong fantasy about her as the perfect wife, and I was telling all my friends that's how I felt about her. So when she told me that she was getting married to someone else, one Saturday morning at her house, I had to leave. I couldn't stay in the same place with her. I had to get out.

I remember driving around aimlessly for hours, not knowing where the hell I was going. I remember that to me my life was shattered at that point. I came home and later on I called her—why I don't know, but I was trying to . . . I was so disbelieving. That was an incredibly frustrating phone call. God knows we talked a lot about it that morning, but I couldn't quite get over it, couldn't quite believe it, and I kept having to get her to repeat it to me, to tell me again, to try and make it more real somehow so I could get over that awful feeling of sheer shock and incredulousness. . . .

I think during that critical day I talked to myself a lot, literally told myself things like, "I must get up and try to behave normally. I must go out and take a walk and go down to pick up my mail and do whatever else it is that I need to do. And so, in a sense, I was living on two levels. There was the normal functional level and the usual effort of being pleasant to people and kids and co-workers and all that, and then there was the second level of having to live with a realization that was almost unbearably painful. Having a good friend that I could spill my guts to helped a lot. I couldn't have gotten through it as well as I did if I hadn't had that. . . .

I feel like I still do want to make a long-term

type of commitment to a woman, and have her make one to me, but I am gun-shy now in a sense. I'm cautious and careful about who I might make a commitment to.

Lately I keep thinking, Oh the hell with that, maybe I should just throw that idea out, not make a commitment to anybody, just have some fun and leave it at that. That's the problem I'm wrestling with now.

Among our major interests in these interviews was to single out some of the chief precursors of relationship failure. The shock that these men felt when the woman announced that she was leaving was often unexpected, but not always. In about half the cases we learned about, it wasn't a complete surprise to him, because his partner had expressed her frustration and unhappiness earlier. But it seemed to us that he must have fatally underestimated the significance of her dissatisfaction, or that she had failed to make it clear enough, to assert it forcefully enough. As a result, somehow both partners had not fully understood the extent of their true estrangement until it was too late. How, we wondered, could this happen? How could it be avoided? What were, in these men's opinions, the most reliable signs of a faltering relationship?

The response of most of our interview participants to these questions was the nebulous identification of "breakdown of communication" as the single most important indicator of impending problems in a relationship. But some of their comments are revealing:

> You know your relationship isn't going well when you don't feel your communication is clear on an intimate level. When one person seems to not need to be in touch with the other any longer, that's definitely a sign that things are going sour, that they don't need or want to be in touch with you.
>
> You need to be able to share feelings honestly

and intimately, something that women seem to have the edge over us on . . . including anger, including, "You really piss me off."

Most men play games, saying things that kind of give clues to what they really mean. They're not talking directly, at least about emotions, especially anger. They're implying things, using innuendo, dropping hints, little things like that. Or they're just clamming up altogether. They feel like they don't have the time to waste on big scenes. But they harbor grudges for long periods of time. Then a month later they drop the bomb: "Why did you keep contradicting me that night when we had dinner at the Harrises and they asked me how I liked 'Apocalypse Now'?" I think it's that kind of grudge-holding and sandbagging behavior in men that makes women paranoid, and makes them feel like if they're going to split, they better do it all at once, all of a sudden.

If you don't get it out, you turn into a walking time bomb, waiting to explode. There needs to be a mutual feeling of confidence about expressing oneself in relationships so that both people know they can really tell the other when they love each other, and when they can't stand what's happening, and why. Not leveling is the problem. Lack of confidence about being able to level with somebody . . .

From my point of view, the kind of thing that happened to me, where a man wakes up one day at age forty-five, in the middle of a marriage that has seemed ideal to him, and suddenly finds his wife is saying, "I've decided this is not for me; I don't want to do this anymore," the kind of shock and desperation that men feel in that situation is a symptom of a lack of communication. It couldn't possibly just take place in an instant, not that kind of radical shift. Unless the ground of the relationship is just filling needs. You might wake up one day and realize that this person is not filling your needs, that might happen suddenly. Or maybe if it's based on wish-fulfillment, on being with someone who subtly helps you maintain a false image of the kind of person you wish you were or hope to be, that could shift overnight too, I guess.

But if it's built on a sense of real communication, which means exposing yourself completely with another person and trusting one another in the middle of that total sense of exposure, then that can't just evaporate overnight. Partly because it's not a thing, or a goal, but a process.

The women to whom we talked tended to refer first to the waning of mutual sexual enthusiasm as a dissolution precursor, and to the appearance of the proverbial wandering eye in their partners. Some agreed that communication breakdown was a sign of impending relationship failure, but it seemed to us that the feminine view of inadequate communication did not exactly coincide with that expressed by the men we spoke to. It may be that there is a failure of communication about communication between the sexes as well.

Naturally it is important to both partners in any relationship to know that expressions of their wishes and complaints have an effect on the other person's attitudes and behavior. If this basic confirmation of personal effectiveness is not forthcoming—whether because issues remain unsolved or because one partner refuses to modify his or her behavior—the normal reaction in both men and women is to feel frustrated and, eventually, powerless. If these feelings continue long enough, they lead to a sense of helplessness and withdrawal.

We suspect that men may be more vulnerable to this sense of verbal powerlessness than women. For whatever reasons, men have, it seems to us, been socialized to assume a more "instrumental" attitude toward their own communications. This is an attitude that assumes that communication is a tool that is intended to have an impact on the actions of others and which is readily judged to have failed if it does not cause perceptible changes in others and in the immediate environment. An alternative interpretation of communication as expressiveness, as emotional catharsis is, due to their "strong but silent" conditioning, relatively foreign to men. Simple emotional ventilation, regardless of its effects, tends to be seen as self-indulgent by them. Thus, we hypothesize that men are more susceptible to the sense of verbal impotence that arises when the same old tired complaint or issue has been aired for the thousandth time and nothing has changed. Men, we suspect, are more personally and deeply affronted when they find that nothing they say really makes a difference any more. And as a consequence, they tend to become emotionally disengaged from communication sooner and more irreversibly than women do.

> It seems to me that women come to the realities of the relationship a lot faster than men. When it's heading into the toilet, when men are feeling insecure, claustrophobic, feeling like they're losing their freedom, that they want to sleep with other women—when men are putting it into the toilet, the woman they're with then will pick it up. Whether the man wants them to, consciously or subconsciously, the woman will pick up on it.
>
> Then for some reason the men go into a state of gray, a mental fuzz. I think it's maybe the double standard at work, a subtle kind of contempt, this state of gray. He thinks she's not going to figure it out, not going to notice that it's going into the toilet, or if she does, he figures she won't dare confront him with it.
>
> But it's more too. Part of what's happening is that the man is trying to get the woman to make

the first move, because he's too guilty to do it himself. This gray state comes in my opinion from being too chickenshit to confront your feelings in the first place, when you realize that it's starting to go down the tubes. Men are terrified of failure.

Women are definitely more emotional than men—not in the sense that they have more emotion, but in the sense that they're more *aware* of their emotions and more willing to confront the emotions that are going on in a situation than ninety percent of most men are. So they call men on it, at least they do now. They don't duck it any more. They aren't just hanging on for dear life and hoping that it will all blow over. . . .

I just had this happen to me for the first time in my life recently. It was the first relationship I've ever been in where the girl walked out on me instead of vice versa. My usual pattern is what you'd call serial monogamy: I live with a woman for three, four, maybe seven years or so, and then something slowly goes sour or something and I leave. I've had three or four relationships like that so far in my life.

This time I was with an older woman, at least in terms of our relative ages. She was eight years older than me, and she has two children. She was very future oriented, was getting herself together, and very involved in her work, and her attitude was, Let's do this relationship right and do it to last; if you're not ready for it, well I am and I'll see you later.

It was strange, ironic maybe, because I started getting closer and closer to her, but she saw through me, saw me for the emotional nomad that I am and saw that she was getting more involved, but she wasn't really heading toward achieving her ultimate goals, wasn't getting the thing worked out in the straightforward, clearcut way she wanted. I guess I started to feel tied down, and I got that gray state going, and brother, she just dumped me. Just said goodbye, told me to move out, and started going out with other guys.

I was devastated. I hadn't had that happen to me before. In a weird way it was cathartic, because I think it's made me more appreciative—in a wary sort of way—of women in general. I mean, I feel burned and I don't want it to happen again.

I was happy to find out that I do have this level of emotion in me, a level that means I can be involved enough to be really hurt by getting dumped, that I'm not an emotional zombie, a basket case, you know, that I could be truly upset and hurt as a result of what a woman did. I mean it's a reassuring kind of vulnerability, once you get over the shock. But the whole thing is still a very touchy subject for me. As far as I'm concerned, women these days are definitely not afraid to take the initiative in cutting it off fast if it's not going where they want it to go.

If there was one thing that men made unmistakably clear to us, one aspect of "communication breakdown" that stood out above all others as causing them the most distress in relationship dissolutions, it was the intense degree to which they resented being put in a non-negotiable position, one in which they have no choice whatsoever but to *react* passively and helplessly to what is presented to them by their partners. In our conversation with Harold Varrick, he made this point vividly and repeatedly:

But to me, that was the worst, the low point, when she said that. Because everything else, anything within the marriage, you can try to work it out. "Well, if we did this differently, if I came home on time, you know, if I took more time with the kids, if you got away more times during the year on your own." You can do all those things, but when someone says, "Look I want to be my own legal entity," there's nothing you can do, but say, "Oh." It's an ultimatum, no matter how gently it's put, and you feel absolutely helpless. . . .

I think I understand it. I mean, I feel like it's been important to me to feel like I'm self-sufficient in some way, psychologically. So I can kind of identify with it, in a way. But to assert it in the middle of a commitment like marriage and a family, to the point of refusing to deal with any kind of counseling, to just absolutely reject any kind of invitation to kind of talk about it, to work it through, to just say, "This is it," and deliver an ultimatum that leaves me with a lot of very difficult, turbulent, painful feelings completely unresolved. That's very hostile and aggressive, to say the least. Sometimes I think it's downright crazy. . . .

Granted, this is a somewhat contradictory complaint to hear from the gender with a strong tendency to retreat from emotional discussions, and to react to frustration in a relationship by becoming silent and withdrawn. But not all men share that predisposition—fewer and fewer, if our interviews are any indication. To give them credit, even those that do are recognizing how truly dependent they have been on their female partners for their persistence in repeatedly raising difficult issues and refusing to let them simply remain ignored. Admitted one of our male respondents:

It's obvious to me that what everyone says about marital discord is true—that the remedy for it is better communication. I for one have never been that much of a talker, and I have never allowed myself to get into a situation where I got so involved with a woman that I would either have to give it up or get down to the emotional brass tacks of what the relationship is all about. I just never let myself get that involved. I went to work, concentrated on my job, and didn't get married until I was thirty-three. And even then, I believe that if I hadn't met Andrea I might never have gotten married at all. She talks, she lets me know what she thinks, what she feels, and if it weren't for the fact that she initiates these probing conversations, which I confess I sometimes find very exhausting, I have to admit that I don't think they ever would have been held at all.

Men are also at a disadvantage in the post-separation adjustment period because of their primary responsibility for instigating the contacts with women that may lead to sexual involvement. A newly single man has to revive his rusty dating skills and prepare himself to risk further rejection by women. Furthermore, the collapse of the previous relationship has often battered a man's self-esteem, making him morbidly sensitive to the prospect of future relationship failures. Many men are economically constrained by the responsibility for maintaining two households and, in many cases, paying alimony or spousal support for some time. Finally, men in this situation are often well into their thirties, forties, or fifties, and are remarkably self-conscious about what they take to be their advanced and thus unattractive age:

I did something when she first told me to drop dead. I went to a couple of singles parties. They're available, if you look for them. I enjoyed myself thoroughly.
And I met some interesting women there. I did this once or twice, but I never pursued it. I don't

know why. I just stopped. I guess I felt very inhibited about bringing a woman back to my apartment. I felt it was too shabby, wasn't nice enough. I guess I'm ashamed of it.

I also felt kind of strange because even though my wife dumped me, she hadn't actually filed for divorce yet then, so when I would meet another woman, an interesting, successful woman, a woman I thought I could like, I felt a little guilty, like I was sailing under false colors, since I was technically still married. I felt like I was cheating, betraying my wife. It's obviously just a very strong conditioned reaction to being married for so long, to being with only one woman, but it's one that's hard to get over.

But even though I felt kinda strange about the whole thing, felt like I didn't know where I stood, I had a very good time. I enjoyed myself thoroughly. I felt this great heady sense of freedom. I kept thinking I don't have to be with my wife anymore, I don't have to think about her, there are all these other wonderful women out there. And they were attractive. I approached about six or seven, and some made it clear they weren't really that interested in me, but some were interested, *very* interested, and I found the whole thing very enjoyable, very interesting, but then I just dropped it.

In fact, in thinking about it now, I think it made me feel absolutely terrified in certain ways. It evoked lots of strong memories of my teens and early twenties, when I was living by myself, going to college, and I was lonely, and miserable, and unhappy, and felt absolutely panicky all the time because I felt so awkward around women. I think what terrifies me is being alone. And I also feel like

I'm too old. I'm forty-three, and most of these women were in their thirties. So that worries me too. That I'm too old for most of them.

And I guess I just worry that I'm not impressive enough somehow, not rich enough, not handsome enough, whatever.

To recapitulate our findings, these interviews left us with the firm impression that, underneath their opaque and unhelpful reticence about the women's movement, men are in fact far more sympathetic to the movement, and far more deeply engaged, at an intellectual and emotional level, with a struggle to come to terms with its perspectives than they are usually given credit for. But it is an embryonic engagement, one that is still characterized by a strong sense of ambivalence and conflict. Men know this, and it tends to make them hesitant to advance their views more emphatically.

Though it is still uninformed, this sense of engagement with women's issues is by no means ingenuous or uncritical. With very few exceptions, the men we spoke to made it clear to us that they did not intend their involvement with these issues to constitute a blanket affirmation of the movement. A sense of integrity forces them to judge each individual concept, program, and sociological critique espoused by the movement on its own merits. Where it seems to make sense to them, not only in terms of their own experience but also in terms of their own liberal desires for a more equitable and just future, they will enthusiastically support it. These men sensed that they have the right—and perhaps the obligation as well—to respond to the proposals of the women's movement carefully, soberly, and deliberately.

IV

Ordeal or Challenge?

So IT SEEMS that men as a group find themselves faced with a complex, difficult, and to some degree unasked-for challenge. The inseparability of the sexes that they have taken more or less for granted now seems far less unquestionable than it used to, and women are far less predisposed to shoulder the responsibility of maintaining the appreciation of reciprocity than they once were. If the interdependence of men and women is to regain and hold a sense of equilibrium in the future, its stability will depend in great part on how actively asserted and deliberately cultivated it is by men.

For more thoughtful and sensitive men this challenge will be an entirely natural and in many ways effortless expansion of the already high level of involvement they have shown in response to the changing role of women. These are men who, rather than feeling threatened by any human quest for greater personal freedom, hold a view of life that acknowledges the inevitability of change. This view not only subscribes to the value of continuous personal growth, but in fact considers it to be fully realizable only through the experiences of intense involvement with another person:

> Now I think it's very clear to me that I like women who are their own person, who are after some substance in their lives. Something with meaning. That's very clear to me. If they don't have that, I'm not as interested in the first place. Second, I could never imagine a long-term relationship with a woman who didn't have that kind of purposefulness to her life. So I gravitate toward that kind of independence in women just automatically. . . .
> I think it's important to be challenged in a relationship. The most important thing is some kind of growth, self-knowledge. That the relationship itself is a challenge to above all explore parts of yourself that are dormant, latent, whatever, parts that need exploring, anyway. Sort of like rooms in your house that you haven't been in in quite a while. That the communication in the relationship is such that it's a mutual exploration of what life is all about, that's important to me. . . .
> I don't think this is a process that has to be shocking. I'm thinking of more of the sort of mutual challenge in the context of a deep friendship, in the sense of not buying into anyone else's trip. And also sort of gently pushing back the edges of that person's habits, stuck places, fixations, belief systems. If it's only a one-way process it doesn't work. I just generally lose interest in those relationships. I don't want to always be the one doing the exploring, I want it to be done to me too, to have someone else play the gently challenging role I'm talking about.

> That seems like the only valid basis for a long-term relationship nowadays, if you can both do that for each other, and, by pushing your communication out into those areas that are new, keep living in new territory all the time, keep the relationship fresh.
>
> It's sort of like circulating fresh air. It has to be a mutual process though, which naturally means that the woman has to be equally strong and has to respect her own intelligence and has to have her own sense of what her life is all about.

Our experiences in preparing this book have convinced us that there are far more men like this around than is usually conceded. Their attitude toward the women's movement may still tend to be cautious, somewhat uninformed, and often tinged with understandable skepticism, but we see no signs whatsoever that they are fighting the panicky resistance action they are often accused of:

> For, however theoretically men may call for "women's liberation" in any social order they may devise, however much they consciously may wish for an end to sexual caste, they still live in the unacknowledged cave of their own subjectivity, their denied fears and longings, and few men can bear to confront that shadow world.[1]
>
> —Adrienne Rich

On the contrary, for those who care to look for them dispassionately, there are abundant signs that for many men the women's movement has represented a welcome opportunity rather than a threat. As one of the men we spoke with recalled:

> One thing that really turns me on now in the city where I live is to see men carrying infants. I see a lot more now than I did even three or four years

ago, all over. The other day I saw one down on Tenth Street—a real brawny sailor, in uniform, with huge muscles, walking along with one of those carrier contraptions that holds the baby in front, against your chest, kind of like a sling. He was just walking along, doing what he wanted to do, not really paying any attention to the kid, but you could see right away he had a little infant in there—you could just see its head and arms and legs sticking out.

And that man looked *so* happy. He was walking down the street and he looked really proud. It makes me feel good when I see that. Fathers taking care of their little kids. No mother in sight. And the kid was probably just as pleased as the father, because he could sense the way the father was feeling.

In some ways, it is regrettable that these men, those whom one might label the masculine counterpart to the effectively radicalized woman, are as inconspicuous as they are. Because they quite rightly cherish the privacy of their individual arrangements with women, it is precisely these men, those who are least likely to form nonrepressive relationships with women, who are overlooked in the gender debate.

Unfortunately, there is also ample evidence that for many other men—those one might call repressively *conditioned*—the women's movement is still highly problematical and fundamentally threatening. News reports daily corroborate the tendency of such men to react to frustration and estrangement, particularly sexual estrangement, with mindless, violent aggression.

In their interviews and casual conversations with us, women made it clear that even minor expressions of male sexual hysteria, expressions that far more commonly take the form of unwanted suggestion, insinuation, and emotional manipulation than outright violence, are still common in their interaction

Ordeal or Challenge?

with men. They also made it clear that, regardless of what form it may take, the nature of the sexual pressuring that men subject women to, particularly when its overtones are those of demand and intimidation rather than invitation, provokes extremely deep resentment in them. Said one woman to us:

> I still find that many men tend to come on to me in a very heavy handed way—you know, the arm draped casually over the shoulder, the shit-eating grin, that sort of thing. I guess that kind of thing has always happened to me, but what's different now is that I'm much more aware than I ever was before of how furious it makes me to have any man, especially one I don't know very well, automatically assume it's alright with me if he wants to come on to me at that level.

Added another woman:

> Men have almost no conception of just how furious women get when they realize that they've been brainwashed by this society into playing the paralyzed rabbit to male sexuality. It really is a humiliating experience to go to bed with someone simply because you haven't got the guts to say no. It's like you're suddenly in a trance, completely helpless, unable to do a damn thing but go along with it. Let me tell you, afterward you feel *depressed*. You feel victimized by the kind of socialization that makes you become a sexual thing, so that some man can exploit you. Underneath it all, men haven't changed. They're still relating to sex as a ripoff, that they've got to put one over on women to get what they want. I mean, can you wonder that women are so angry at men?
>
> Underneath all this superficial hype about permissiveness and sexual freedom and being up front

is that same old heavy-handed, desperate masculine trip. I mean, I have to laugh, men are so damn transparent, such hypocrites. They learn all these new "liberated" moves, but basically it's the same old pressure, the same old hassle. They have got to have it or they'll freak out, you know? I mean that's the message they're really sending. They beg, they flatter, they charm, they all but stand on their hind legs and bark . . . the whole thing is pathetic. But if you don't go along, they get nasty. Why, I had one dude say to me, just recently, "You just don't want to be open." I mean, can you beat that for bullshit! He wants to screw and he's trying to lay this guilt trip on me about it! It's that same old self-absorbed conquest number, where you're a goddess until they've got you where they want you. Then you're a part of the landscape and they forget all about being so enchanted with you.

Underneath it there's a whole lot of manipulation and intimidation going on and women are just basically sick of it. They don't want to make it with some guy whose whole identity is on the line, but they don't want the cool sex machine type either. They just want human beings, friends, warmth and affection straight from the heart, and that's where men really miss the boat, because by and large, they haven't heard a thing that women have been telling them.

Commented a third woman:

Actually I think the most impressive insight I've gained into the sexism of this culture has come from reading the books that have come out recently about rape. Susan Brownmiller's book,

Against Our Will, and Susan Griffin's, *Rape and the Power of Consciousness.*

The Brownmiller book is written very objectively, in my opinion. Almost anthropologically. Susan Griffin is the only woman I've read—I think her first article came out some twelve, fourteen years ago now—who's written about how pervasive the *threat* of rape is in this culture and what that threat, even more than the actual act, does to a woman's consciousness. And maybe men's too, I suppose.

I guess the basic point in it is that rather than being a sexual act, rape is really more an act of aggression, of violence, a way of keeping women in line. How its threat makes you afraid to walk down the street or go from one place to another without an escort. It's an intimidation technique.

Maybe the related point about male psychology would be that in relation to the macho mentality, a lot of the aggressiveness that men have traditionally shown toward women actually has more to do with their relation to each other. In that sense, these books are trying to show that rape has to do with property rights, and the assumption is that women are a form of property. So when you rape a woman you're actually damaging another man's property. The worst thing you can do to humiliate a man is to hurt "his" woman, which is still pretty true in this culture. That's why there was the whole premium on virginity until a couple of generations ago. You make a man feel more powerless when he can't protect his property. It makes him feel unmanly, wounds him spiritually.

Women feel rage over all this. I know I do. And I guess some men do too. I know I've had men tell me how awful it is to find that women on the street at night or in halls in buildings jump when they come up behind them unexpectedly. I mean, there's really nothing worse than to have everyone be terrified of you just because of something arbitrary, like your sex, or the color of your skin. It's dehumanizing. I suppose it's another form of prejudice, though it's hardly one you can blame women for.

It is by such actions as rape, beating, and the murder of women that some men reveal the true extent of their estrangement from female (and thus human) emancipation, especially emancipation from the role of sexual compliance and submissiveness. It may have become a truism to observe that beneath the prototypical macho attitude toward sex and women there lies a profound fear of sexual weakness, impotence, and rejection, but it bears repeating that women like those quoted above, no matter how much they may understand this fear, are not about to condone the sexual repressiveness that some men form in defense against it. Placing women in a position where their sexual assent is required as confirmation of virility will only provoke intense resentment from them, and will obliterate any possibility of genuinely erotic arrangements.

It is becoming clear that overabsorption in the traditional masculine role is nonadaptive in other ways as well. Men who feel inhibitions about expressing their frustration and anger outward may internalize it, sometimes in equally repressive and tragic ways:

> • In Ohio, a forty-five-year-old biology professor is told by his wife that she wants to leave him and that she wants custody of their two children. Two weeks later, at a meeting with his lawyer, he pulls a revolver from his briefcase and, mumbling that his "world is crashing in around" him, fires a single shot into his head, dying instantly.

There is, however, a third group of men, composed of those who are neither effectively liberated nor repressively insulated from the women's movement. For this group, which in our view constitutes the major portion of men, the current estrangement between the sexes is only one dimension of a larger sense of estrangement they have faced all their lives: the estrangement between their drives to achieve something meaningful in life, to fulfill what seems to be an inherent human appetite for purposefulness and productivity, with the equally strong but evidently (and painfully) antithetical wish to experience complete erotic union with another being. It is an estrangement between tense, lonely striving—which for men has usually been restricted to the occupational setting—and relaxation into sexual symbiosis, and it is an estrangement that lies at the heart of this culture.

Indirect confirmation of many of the tenets of this argument appear almost daily, most notably in the writings of psychotherapists, especially those who specialize in sexual dysfunction. Over and over again in their comments emerges the theme of male estrangement from a truly erotic appreciation for sexuality.

Herb Goldberg, for example, alludes repeatedly in *The New Male* to the predominant masculine tendency to relate to sex as if it were a mechanical, goal-oriented process:

> The traditionally conditioned male is so disconnected from the emotions attached to his sexual response that when he is not performing sexually as he believes he should be, he disclaims his response by denying responsibility. Specifically, he curses his penis for not performing, as he sweats and strains and informs his partner that *he* really wants to, even though something seems to be wrong with *it*. He is relating to his penis as if it were a piece of machinery that has become faulty but that has no connection with his feelings about or desire for his partner.

Because he does not perceive his penis as an expression of his feeling but rather as a separate mechanism with a will of its own, when it "malfunctions," his inclination is to get "it" fixed as quickly as possible.[2]

The traditionally conditioned male must be sexually in jeopardy because his entire early conditioning process creates the basis for him to become a psychological stranger to himself and his sexual responses. . . .
From early boyhood on, his sensuality is repressed. Hugging, kissing, touching, stroking, being close and engaging in body play were not considered masculine. Indulgence in them, in fact, made him suspect of being a "sissy." Consequently, as an adult, he approaches sex as a goal-oriented activity, rather than a playful, sensual interchange in which the process of lovemaking is the major source of pleasure and satisfaction.[3]

Dr. Helen Singer Kaplan, author of *The New Sex Therapy*, has recently commented at some length on what she describes as a "highly prevalent" fear of erotic intimacy in contemporary American society, one that she has labeled "sexual anorexia." Reporting at the Eastern Regional Conference of the Society for the Scientific Study of Sex, Kaplan notes that sexual anorexia, which may affect individuals of both sexes and from the entire spectrum of socioeconomic backgrounds, is often attributable to stress.

Intimacy describes a special quality of emotional closeness between two people.
It is an affectionate bond, the strands of which are composed of mutual caring, responsibility, trust, open communication of feelings and sensa-

tions, as well as the nondefined interchange of information about significant emotional events.

The prototype of intimacy is the maternal-infant bond, wherein the caring mother is constantly alert and responsive to the infant's feeling tone, to the fluctuations of the emotional currents of her baby.

Intimacy is an important ingredient in the quality of love and life.

A high degree of intimacy between two lovers or spouses contributes to the happiness and emotional stability of both.

All activities are more enjoyable and life is richer and more colorful when shared with an intimate partner.[4]

Remarking that "there is no doubt humans were meant to live in pairs," Kaplan also observes that "fear of intimacy . . . may produce problems that extend beyond sexual dysfunctions . . . Without intimate relationships, we tend to get lonely and depressed . . . The availability of intimate relationships is an important determinant of how well we master life's crises."

In couples where both individuals are afflicted with sexual anorexia, a pattern commonly develops, according to Kaplan, where the partners "long for closeness with each other, but when they achieve a certain point of contact, they become anxious. Then one or the other will behave in such a manner as to create a distance."

Nothing, however, more grimly underscores the predominantly male susceptibility to repressive de-eroticization, to use Herbert Marcuse's famous phrase, than a report by Caroline Huffine and Warren Breed in *The Psychopathology of Aging*, that men in their mid-seventies are *seven* times more likely than women of the same age to commit suicide.[5] Why? According to Huffine and Breed it is because the same qualities that work so well for men during their working years—drive, ambition, a perfectionistic and compulsive need to achieve—all these traits lead them to become rigid and inflexible, and to subordinate their all-important adaptive (i.e., erotic?) skills to the search for "mastery over the environment."

When retirement brings a sudden loss of purposeful endeavor, and an end to many "rewarding" occupational relationships and the source of a sense of accomplishment, these men cannot tolerate what they experience as a crushing sense of failure and loss. They have suddenly lost the only libidinal gratifications they had, those that were systematically included in the world of work, and they find themselves suddenly estranged from even these gratifications, in a sense rejected and abandoned in an alien and repressively de-eroticized world.

Huffine and Breed suggest that the comparatively low suicide rate among older women is explained by their greater adaptability and better coping skills. Women, they point out, learn how to make role shifts throughout their lives, as they move from employee to mother to wife to lover to friend, and so on. For most men, although their lives change, the major role change of their lives is from worker to retiree, and too often they find it an intolerable loss. These men have become so identified with a technological mode of realization of their fundamentally erotic "life instincts" that when they are suddenly separated from them, they behave in an entirely consistent manner: They die.

As women become more and more deeply involved with the world of work, many women are beginning to exhibit some of the same "de-eroticized" traits associated with the traditional masculine role. In Dr. Doreen Schecter's words, they are becoming "robotlike, mechanical or dead . . . Such luxuries as love and intimacy, trust and genuine commitment to another human being or to one's work have no survival in our current cultural 'success ethos' . . . In many relationships, a defensive invulnerability thus becomes a badge of honor, worn to spite the partner."[6]

In many ways, the special dilemma of men—and increasingly of women—is to find ways to fulfill what has traditionally been defined as a typical and exclusively masculine need for a sense of significant purpose—that which Margaret Mead has described as "irreversible achievement" and which Steven Goldberg has analyzed as an historically (and perhaps genetically triggered) masculine drive for attainment and "dominance"—but to do so in a way that does not perpetuate their alienation from the mutually nourishing effects of a more richly erotic interdependence with others.

Frustration at failing to find or develop a satisfactory sense of larger purpose may well also be one of the many factors contributing to the remarkably higher differences—a difference that is closing fast in some areas—between male and female morbidity and mortality figures for such typical stress-related disorders as ulcer, colitis, emphysema, diabetes, pancreatitis, allergy, hypertension, cardiovascular disease, and possibly even certain kinds of cancer. The longing to burn brighter, men have found, can simply pose the risk of burning out sooner.

Men of this third group who recognize these signs of estrangement in themselves can and should do something about them. Failing to act, to respond to one's own self-diagnosis of detachment, dissatisfaction, and lack of fully effective self-integration will only evoke feelings of helplessness and futility, which will in turn only aggravate the symptoms of essential estrangement. We can't presume to offer prescriptions that will be applicable to every man's unique, individual conditions—each man will have to determine those for himself—but we can offer a general description of what we take to be a few of the major zones of turbulence in most men's lives, particularly in terms of the gender controversy.

First, for most men, revitalization of their erotic sensibilities will continue to be a function of a lasting, wholehearted, more or less monogamous arrangement with a woman. This in turn means, given the powerful influence in recent years of the women's movement on women's consciousnesses, that men who haven't already done so would be well advised to relinquish whatever inclination they may still feel to dismiss the women's movement as a transient aberration of some kind, one that will eventually subside into cultural oblivion, leaving traditional gender arrangements fundamentally intact and allowing a traditional form of male pre-eminence to reemerge. They should also avoid a show of generous (but in fact devoutly indifferent) compliance with the movement's more "rational" and "objective" proposals—an attempt to placate women and to forestall further escalation of their demands. Such a strategy will not work.

As the current revolution in traditional sex roles continues to progress, passive resistance to more active participation in it, refusal on the part of men to assert their right to an equal place in helping to determine its course of development, will be interpreted less and less as a simple statement of indifference or ignorance and more and more as a sign of tacit obstructiveness. The once feasible attitude of helpful but detached sympathy, of neutral ratification of the aims and values of the women's movement has become steadily less acceptable to women energetically pursuing their own self-liberation, according to those we talked to. Too many men chronically underestimate the extent to which even those women (probably the majority, in our opinion) who are unwilling to declare a formal allegiance to feminism nevertheless consider this commonplace masculine attitude of "objective" but fundamentally noncommittal sanction of the movement's aims to be nothing more than complacent and patronizing.

Until a man can acknowledge that the women's movement, in exerting an irrevocable influence on women, has therefore already exerted a strong if as yet unanalyzed effect on men as well, he will be obliged to accommodate whatever changes in his role follow as a necessary and logical consequence of the changed roles of the women he becomes involved with. He will, as interviewee Harold Varrick put it in Chapter III, be forced to continue to *react to* rather than to initiate many of the major changes in his life.

This acknowledgement of the women's movement will become doubly important if, as we anticipate, the women's movement is only now entering the second phase of its current renaissance, a phase in which many of its more theoretical proposals will be brought down to earth in practical, *effective* economic and political programs dealing with the ordinary problems ordinary women face daily. Ideally, what the women's movement becomes in this second phase, as it expands and consolidates its gains of the past two decades, will be far more a function of an extensive and outspoken response to it by effectively radicalized men. Only through such a response will the movement's espousal of fundamentally humanistic, erotic bases and objectives be realized.

There is copious evidence that men generally tend to discount, override, and just plain ignore what women *are* saying to them, no matter how revolutionary it may be. Study after study in recent years has concluded that the male conversational role, particularly in interactions with women, is one of constant, one-way verbal broadcast, with very little room left for reception. Men dominate these conversations, they do not follow up on the topical leads that women give them, and they interrupt. According to University of Arizona sociology professor Lois Mohr, "One study done at professional conferences found that men spent twice as much time asking a question as women spent . . . Males have fewer pauses and much more overlap in their conversations. With women there are a lot more pauses, which means they're reflecting on what the person has said. When there are overlaps, it means people aren't listening."[7] Various studies place the percentage of interrupting that is done by males in male-female conversations at anywhere from sixty percent to ninety percent. As *Christian Science Monitor* columnist Melvin Maddocks has commented, it seems at times that men "not only don't know what women mean, they don't especially want to find out."

As a natural result of these steps, we also believe that men will inevitably become much more explicit about what they believe a renewed sense of masculinity to be, about what its values and characteristic traits are, and about what it represents. Much of the exasperating reticence on the part of men in response to the women's movement stems from sheer confusion over the meaning of a changing sense of masculinity. Men may tend to accept the feminist critique of masculinity, to agree that traditional gender roles have been based on discriminatory expectations of attitude and behavior patterns, and that they deserve readjustment, but men do *not*, by and large, accept the argument that masculinity and femininity—that gender differentiation *per se*—is an outmoded and repressive distinction. Gender differentiation remains an indisputable fact to most men, even as they struggle to accommodate the baffling display of gender expressions that currently preoccupies our society, and to develop an understanding of what precisely it is that the term "masculinity" is coming to stand for.

Furthermore, men are also increasingly sensitive to the fact that their resistance to defining their individual perspectives on masculinity is in and of itself a vestige of an era when men had no need to articulate their role because it was never subject to question and re-evaluation.

Forty years ago, perhaps less, if you were a man it pretty much didn't matter what you did, within very broad limits, as long as you were a responsible provider and protector. You could drink, play, gamble, sleep on the couch all day on Sunday, even womanize a little, discreetly, because your obligations, as a man, were entirely fulfilled by meeting your function as provider and protector. A tacit but powerful social contract prevailed, one in which the male role was more or less exempted from social assessment in exchange for his support of a wife and family.

Unfortunately, few men realized, because it was highly implicit, how strong a reciprocal dependence on women there was in this role, a dependence that has only recently become highly visible, largely because the women's movement has succeeded in bringing it into such vivid focus. The traditional male role presupposed a certain pattern of behavior and aspirations on the part of women, and only as long as women were in tacit collusion with this presupposition—as most in fact were—could it continue. As long as women too felt they were getting what they needed and wanted from life, the traditional male role could not legitimately be regarded as oppressive.

Nor, by the same token, could traditional masculine compliance with the expectation that he would sacrifice the greater part of his adult life to working to provide for the material well-being of his wife and children be considered repressive. Man was neither oppressor nor oppressed, but symbiotic, complementary, interdependent partner to woman. His sacrifices were validated by hers. Her constraints, conversely, were justified by his. She provided the foil for his sense of significance in his life, and he served the same function for her. There was, though it may now be viewed as unequal, a functional, pragmatic, viable partnership in effect.

When women served notice on men in the last few years that this arrangement no longer suits them, much of the meaning of the traditional masculine role was automatically forfeit. For the regeneration of a sense of partnership between men and women, on a more equal basis, the value of masculinity must first be reaffirmed and its meaning redefined, but this time without reference to subservient female roles. Men quite obviously cannot presume any longer to speak for women, but in order to speak effectively *to* women it is also clear that they are first going to have to learn how to speak more expansively about themselves.

In short, men will no longer be able to fulfill their sense of gender identity through the simple fact of supporting a family. They undoubtedly *will* continue to support, or help support, their families, but this role alone will no longer serve to satisfy the human quest of most men for a sense of self-esteem. The role of provider and protector will no longer suffice as the *sine qua non* of masculine pride.

What will? We don't know, and we doubt that anyone else does either at the moment. At its most basic level, it will be the challenge of every individual man to make this decision for himself.

The effect of all this transformation in the male role has been to place men in a peculiar and unprecedented bind. In order to reclaim the sense of natural partnership with women that they have lost, men now have to undertake a problematical venture:

Each one must turn inward in order to understand and recapture his unique appreciation for masculinity, but he must, paradoxically, do so without allowing this new and in most respects healthy introspection to be transformed into narcissistic self-absorption, and thus even more pronounced withdrawal and even more counterproductive detachment and reticence.

Men who accept this challenge and undertake this venture, men who assume the risks of looking awkward and clumsy as they venture candidly into the terra incognita of the masculine ethos, and who are yet able to retain a sense of masculine pride, vigor, and humor at the same time will, we suspect, be in the vanguard of the process of shaping a new model of masculine valor.

In our culture, masculine purposefulness is closely associated with hero myths, and most men, even today, are still imbued with incorrigibly romantic notions of self-sufficiency, honor, and noble sacrifice in service to others. Within even the most pragmatic male breast there beats, we believe, the heart of a would-be hero. As Dr. Wolfgang Lederer has suggested, even some of our most contemporary concepts partake of the romantic legacy of the hero.

> The Romans had a word for manliness: *virtus*—hence our "virtue." And the most manly of virtues has always been courage, and the model, the prototype of manliness, has always been the hero. For almost all of human history kids grew up on hero tales, and shaped their ego ideal accordingly. Freud grew up on hero tales, as did his early followers, such as Rank and Jung. They never tired of the heroic paradigm, and they continually derived new meanings from it.
>
> Courage is, in and of itself, an exhilarating virtue. Courageous action may not always make us happy, but it is bound to create a deep sense of pride and satisfaction. Heroism is courage in the service of someone or something else; it is tran-

scendence of the self for the sake of service. As such it is the very opposite of narcissism.[8]

Unfortunately, there are fewer and fewer dragons around to slay (though perhaps more and more windmills left to tilt at) in this highly technological, extremely materialistic, impossibly egocentric age. And now the damsels are, quite understandably, refusing to play distressed, and are declining *en masse* to wait around to be saved. Instead of jousts and crusades, men face commutes, committees, and, according to Herbert Marcuse, calculated manipulation of their libidos.

To some extent the rise of a technological age is probably a healthy and certainly an irrevocable development. But it places men in a precarious position, psychologically, regardless of how well they may be doing materially. Unless men can shift the focus of their deep purposeful drives from material attainment to psychological integration, those very same drives will tend to deteriorate into ennui, loneliness, self-absorption, sentimentalized detachment from social involvement, and self-pitying estrangement from erotic intimacy with a significant other.

Traditionally the affirmation of masculinity in America has proceeded in estrangement from society and others, an estrangement that our culture has unabashedly romanticized in its archetypal images of the hero. The New World hero has always been the man who acts instead of talks, and who acts on his own. "I've always acted alone," said Henry Kissinger to Oriana Fallaci. "Americans admire that enormously. Americans admire the cowboy leading the caravan astride his horse, the cowboy entering a village or city alone on his horse."

By flatly rejecting the secondary, supporting role that the mythology of the hero so rigidly cast them in, the women's movement has exposed the hypocrisy that maintained it: the tacit assumption that the hero's isolation was also self-sufficiency, that he had no basic need of friends, family, or community, that his true strength derived from his ability to deny deep involvement with others.

By unilaterally withdrawing their support for this myth,

women have traumatically revealed to men the true extent of the now problematic interdependence between the sexes, an interdependence that some women are themselves in danger of underestimating. In our opinion, it would be truly unfortunate, if having precipitated this powerful revelation, effectively radicalized women were to blind themselves to the unavoidable corollary, that neither gender can afford to pursue its future in isolation from the other; struggling to do so will only compound the alienation of the illusory myth of the hero.

The dissociation of gender from any preconceived functions, roles, or obligations is an unshakable advance. Like any great radical reform, it has helped free us all from the unseen limitations of preconceptions. But by the same token, in loosing the bonds of an unjust past, it has left us all adrift in a cultural vacuum. Now that we grasp once again the extent and depth of our gender interdependence, we need to reassert it, to reconnect man with other, man with community, man with woman.

The challenge that men face is also a particularly painful one because the idea of asserting one's masculinity has been so thoroughly discredited that men cannot readily and unilaterally re-evoke the rapport with women, the gender inseparability, that they have presupposed before and that they now feel bereft of. Masculine independence, once idealized as a thrilling and even noble condition, now tastes only bitter. It has become an ordeal of estrangement.

This is the heart of the challenge that men now face, to reaffirm a courageous purposefulness that is uniquely masculine, to reclaim a sense of masculine dignity and pride, but to do so without making assumptions of any kind about women and their roles.

This will be a demanding task, since it will inevitably expose men to their own intrinsic confusion about masculinity and its values, and will make them feel self-conscious and peculiarly vulnerable. The typically masculine temptation to saddle up and ride out of town will be hard to resist.

It will take a special kind of courage for men to reclaim the emotional integration that is their human birthright and that their past roles have tended to exclude them from. It will be a new kind of masculine courage that admits to feeling emotionally awkward as it struggles to reconnoiter a psychological terra incognita, a fearlessness that admits to pain and fear, shame and humiliation as it returns again to forgotten lands that men have been led, by their images of themselves, to forget.

Notes

Preface

1. Germaine Greer, *People*, December 17, 1979, p. 102.
2. Dorothy Dinnerstein, *The Mermaid and the Minotaur: Sexual Arrangements and Human Malaise*, New York: Harper & Row, 1976, p. 274.

I The Male Dilemma

1. *Newsweek*, January 16, 1978, p. 55.
2. Pierre Mornell, M.D., *Passive Men, Wild Women*, New York: Simon and Schuster, 1979.
3. *Newsweek*, January 16, 1978, p. 61.

II Studying and Portraying Men's Reactions to the Women's Movement

1. Herb Goldberg, *The Hazards of Being Male: Surviving the Myth of Masculine Privilege*, New York: Signet, 1976, p. 10.

2. Ellen Halle, "The Abandoned Husband: When Wives Leave," *Psychiatric Opinion*, Vol. 16, No. 10, November/December 1979, p. 18.
3. Ellen Halle, *Psychiatric News*, Vol. 14, July 6, 1979, pp. 18–19.
4. Goldberg, *The Hazards of Being Male*, pp. 172–173.
5. Darla Welles, Copley News Service, March 5, 1980.
6. Adrienne Rich, *Of Woman Born*, New York: Bantam, 1976, p. 65.
7. Gloria Steinem, Introduction to *The Male Machine*, Marc Feigen Fasteau, New York: Delta, 1975, pp. xiv–xv.
8. Betty Friedan, reported by Richard Reeves, *San Francisco Chronicle*, August 27, 1979.
9. Marilyn French, *The Women's Room*, New York: Jove, 1978, pp. 287–288.
10. Dinnerstein, p. 272.

III Men Respond: The Interviews

1. Hoffman Reynolds Hays, *The Dangerous Sex: The Myth of Feminine Evil*, New York: G. P. Putnam's Sons, 1964, p. 18.
2. Eric Hoffer, *The True Believer*, New York: Harper and Brothers, 1951, p. 108.
3. Ibid., p. 93.
4. Ibid., p. 94.
5. Marilyn French, *The Women's Room*, p. 290.
6. Phyllis Chesler, *Women and Madness*, New York: Avon, 1973, p. 75.
7. Shulamith Firestone, *The Dialectic of Sex: The Case for Feminist Revolution*, New York: Bantam, 1970, pp. 126–127.
8. UPI, November 25, 1979.
9. Herb Goldberg, *The New Male: From Self-Destruction to Self-Care*, New York: Morrow, 1979, p. 289: see also pp. 236–249.

10. Marc Feigen Fasteau, *The Male Machine*, New York: Delta, 1975, p. 45.
11. Goldberg, *New Male*, pp. 151–152, 212–213; see also Goldberg's *The Hazards of Being Male: Surviving the Myth of Masculine Privilege*, New York: Signet, 1976, pp. 5–7.
12. Wolfgang Lederer, M.D., "The Decline of Manhood: Adaptive Trend or Temporary Confusion?" *Psychiatric Opinion*, Vol. 16, No. 10, November/December 1979, p. 16.
13. Goldberg, *New Male*, p. 193.
14. Richard M. Restak, M.D., *The Brain: The Last Frontier*, Garden City, New York: Doubleday, 1979.
15. Ibid., p. 202.
16. Fasteau, *The Male Machine*, p. 45.
17. Dinnerstein, *The Mermaid and the Minotaur*, p. 7.
18. John Money, "Matched Pairs of Hermaphrodites: Behavioral Biology of Sexual Differentiation from Chromosomes to Gender Identity," *Engineering and Science*, Vol. 33, No. 34, Calfiornia Institute of Technology, 1970; Special Issue: *Biological Bases of Human Behavior*; cited in Steven Goldberg, *The Inevitability of Patriarchy*, London: Maurice Temple Smith, 1977, p. 93.
19. Fasteau, *Male Machine*, p. 196.
20. Chesler, *Women and Madness*, p. 98.
21. Fasteau, *Male Machine*, p. 76.
22. Hays, *The Dangerous Sex*; Lederer, *The Fear of Women*, New York: Harcourt Brace Jovanovich, 1968; Dinnerstein, *The Mermaid and the Minotaur*.
23. Nancy Friday, *Time*, February 18, 1980, p. 50.
24. Goldberg, *New Male*, pp. 140–141.
25. Fasteau, *Male Machine*, p. 22.
26. Graham B. Spanier and Randie Margolis, "Marital Quality, Marital Stability, and Extramarital Sexual Behavior," paper presented at the annual meeting of the International Academy of Sex Research, August 21, 1979, Prague, Czechoslovakia.
27. Ibid., p. 9.

28. Ibid., pp. 11–12.
29. Ibid.; see also Herb Goldberg's detailed comments on more or less the same phenomenon in *The Hazards of Being Male*, pp. 122–125.
30. George F. Gilder, *Sexual Suicide*, New York: Quadrangle, 1973, pp. 63–64.
31. Jessie Bernard, *The Future of Marriage*, New York: Bantam, 1973, p. 19.
32. *Time*, March 17, 1980, p. 65.
33. Dinnerstein, *The Mermaid and the Minotaur*, p. 34.

IV Ordeal or Challenge?

1. Adrienne Rich, *Of Woman Born: Motherhood as Experience and Institution*, New York: Bantam, 1976, p. 69.
2. Goldberg, *The New Male*, pp. 119–120.
3. Ibid., p. 123.
4. Tricia McCormack, UPI, November 12, 1979.
5. Oscar J. Kaplan, ed., *The Psychopathology of Aging*, New York: Academic Press, 1980.
6. Doreen E. Schecter, M.D., "Women in the Labor Force: Some Mental Health Implications," *Psychiatric Opinion*, Vol. 16, No. 8, September 1979, pp. 17–19.
7. Dan Huff, Gannett News Service, December 11, 1979.
8. Lederer, "The Decline of Manhood," pp. 14–17.

A Reading List for Men

Dinnerstein, Dorothy, *The Mermaid and the Minotaur: Sexual Arrangement and Human Malaise*, New York: Harper & Row, 1976.
Fasteau, Marc Feigen, *The Male Machine*, New York: Delta, 1975.
Fensterheim, Herbert and Jean Baer, *Don't Say Yes When You Want to Say No*, New York: Dell, 1975.
Friedman, Meyer, M.D., and Ray H. Rosenman, M.D., *Type A Behavior and Your Heart*, Greenwich, Conn.: Fawcett Crest, 1974.
Gilder, George F., *Sexual Suicide*, New York: Quadrangle, 1973.
Goldberg, Herb, *The Hazards of Being Male: Surviving the Myth of Masculine Privilege*, New York: Signet, 1977.
Goldberg, Herb, *The New Male: From Self-Destruction to Self-Care*, New York: Morrow, 1979.
Goldberg, Steven, *The Inevitability of Patriarchy*, London: Maurice Temple Smith, Ltd., 1977.
Hays, Hoffman, R., *The Dangerous Sex: The Myth of Feminine Evil*, New York: G. P. Putnam's Sons, 1964.
Schoenfeld, Eugene, M.D., *Jealousy: Taming the Green-Eyed Monster*, New York: Holt, Rinehart and Winston, 1980.

Seligman, Martin E. P., *Helplessness: On Depression, Development, and Death*, San Francisco: W. H. Freeman, 1975.

Shaevitz, Marjorie Hansen and Morton H. Shaevitz, *Making It Together as a Two-Career Couple*, Boston: Houghton Mifflin, 1980.